I'd Love To Tell The World

Compiled by
Harold J. Westing

ACCENT BOOKS
Denver, Colorado

MEMBER OF
EVANGELICAL CHRISTIAN
PUBLISHERS ASSOCIATION

ACCENT BOOKS
12100 W. Sixth Avenue
P.O. Box 15337
Denver, colorado 80215

Library of Congress Catalog Card Number: 77-075131
ISBN O-916406-67-9

Meet the Authors

HAROLD WESTING, who did the organizational work in compiling this book presenting the challenge of missions to this generation, has been active in Christian Education, serving in various capacities for over twenty years. He served as director of Christian Education for several large churches in Oregon, Director of Christian Education for the state of Oregon for the Conservative Baptist Association and as national director of Christian Education for the same denomination. He is the author of numerous articles and books and is now teaching on the faculty of the Conservative Baptist Theological Seminary in Denver as an assistant professor of Christian Education.

FLOYD MC ELVEEN, and his wife Virginia, ministered their first term as missionaries in Cooper Landing on Kenai Peninsula in southern Alaska. Later they served in other locations, including Anchorage, always working where a church was needed and moving on when the church became self-supporting. The McElveens are now continuing the new church ministry in Idaho.

WARREN WEBSTER worked for 17 years in Muslim evangelism and a literature ministry in West Pakistan. Both he and his wife Shirley being schooled in linguistics, developed alphabets for the first literature ever published in the Marwari and Odki languages and also worked on the revision of the Sindhi New Testament. Much of his work with the Muslims was carried on through Bible correspondence courses and he served as editor and consultant for two Christian literature societies publishing in different languages. Dr. Webster is presently General Director of the foreign mission society he serves.

NORMAN WETTHER carried a burden for the spiritual needs of servicemen ever since his own service in the Army. He was not surprised when he and his wife Joyce were appointed to serve on Guam in 1956, where they established an active Christian Servicemen's Center and a Baptist church. In 1970, he became the liason between his mission and missionaries serving in North and Central America, the West Indies Islands, and U.S. Possessions.

CHARLES GREEN, and his wife Jo Helene, began their missionary service in 1962 in Northern Argentina. During their years of service there they lived in Tartagal, San Pedro and Salta, establishing seven churches. He taught for a time in the San Pedro seminary. Due to medical reasons, the Greens returned to the United States and are now conducting a new churches program in northwest New Mexico.

BRUCE KER, who was born to missionary parents in Ceylon, served with his wife Esther first in the Philippine Islands, working in a student ministry, theological education and church planting. Later, when visas unexpectedly became available for them, they transferred to

Ceylon and entered into preaching, church conference work, church planting and in education at Colombo Bible College. Dr. Ker transferred to Hong Kong when the door to Ceylon was closed, teaching in Hong Kong Bible Seminary and Hong Kong Bible College. He is now Dean of student affairs and assistant professor of Missions at Western Conservative Baptist Theological Seminary in Portland, Oregon.

RICHARD LINDEMANN and his wife Julie were in missionary service for four years in South Brazil in the city of Piraciacaba. To reach students attending the city's university and twelve colleges, he started Bible clubs among the students and trained more than 25 student leaders through these clubs to reach others with the gospel of Christ. He now serves his mission as an area representative.

MARJORIE SHELLEY who began her missionary work in Congo, now Zaire, is director of the Evangelical Publications Center in Ivory Coast, Africa. She holds a master's degree in religious education and one in journalism and has been awarded a Doctor of Divinity degree. Under her direction nationals and missionaries produce Bible teaching literature which is distributed widely in French speaking Africa. Echo du Tam-Tam, a magazine for children and Champion, a magazine for youth, reach into many African countries presenting the message of Christ. She directs the publication of tracts, Sunday School materials, and Christian books and also conducts writing workshops in various countries seeking to develop African Christian writers.

GEORGE PATTERSON, and his wife Mardalene, realized the need for missionary work when his duties in connection with his army assignment in Japan included supervising youth activities for teenage children of U.S. Army personnel. This included joint programs with the Japanese youth. They have served in Honduras since 1964. He works in connection with the Honduras Bible Institute located in Olanchito. He has been working in an extension program of training a group of nationals who in turn go to key centers to teach others. Through this program many national-led Bible studies are now scattered over Honduras—the seed for planting future Bible-believing churches.

LOIS MORDEN has served in Brazil with her husband Hubert who directed a theological seminary in Floriano, Brazil. Mrs. Morden taught in the seminary, was organist for the seminary choir and has written three books on music which have been widely used in Brazil. She also co-authored the book, Panorama of the Bible which was published in Portuguese.

RALPH COVELL, with his wife Ruth, served as a missionary in China from 1946 until missionaries were evacuated in 1951. Then he transferred his missionary efforts to Taiwan where he helped with the theological training of national church leaders. During this time he also translated the New Testament into one of the tribal languages. Dr. Covell is now professor of missions at the Denver seminary.

Contents

CHAPTER 1

Why a Life Commitment?

Floyd McElveen

It was a cold, rainy, sleety day in the little village of Copper Landing, Alaska, especially up on the roof of a log church where we were working. We were 'rigid with the frigid'! Suddenly, Uncle Harley, a 63-year-old choice saint of God, slipped and slid to the very edge of the roof. Recovering just in time, he took the ladder to the ground, where he stood shaking and quaking.

"Uncle Harley, how does it feel to be on terra firma?" I called.

"The more firma, the less terror!" he retorted, quick as a flash.

It is odd that so many who see themselves as being firmly in Christ seem to react with something approaching terror when we talk about life commitment. Why a life commitment?

Well, why not?

The Call of God for Salvation and Service

Let's consider "The Call of God for Salvation and Service."

Calls are compelling, intense, interesting. Consider the soft, ineffably sweet cooing of a wooing dove for its mate. My boys and I have reveled in Alaska to the querulous call of the loon in the wilderness. The bugle of a bull elk is challenging, thrilling. The call of a wolfpack, all around one on a cold, crisp Alaskan night is spine-tingling, unforgettable. One of the most poignant calls I have ever heard was the call of a woman dying from multiple injuries in a car wreck, calling urgently for her husband who had already bled to death.

Far beyond and above any of these calls, however, is a call more loving, more challenging, more intense, more beautiful, and more compelling. It is the call of God by His Holy Spirit to respond heart and soul to Christ.

First, we are called to look at bloody, terrible, magnificant Calvary, to God the Son, thirsty, wounded, dying, for me—for you. There is no greater call, no greater love. We are called to commit ourselves *unreservedly* to Christ, because there He died in our place.

Then, we are called via the empty tomb to share in His resurrection life. And immediately, as Acts 1:8 explicitly declares, each of us is empowered, impressed, and impassioned by the Holy Spirit, as well as commanded by His Word, *to share Him everywhere.*

Now consider this. We are "bought with a price," as I Corinthians 6:20 tells us, obviously the precious blood of Christ, as Colossians 1:14 affirms: "In whom we have redemption through his blood, even the forgiveness of sins." Then who has the right to us and our services?

Suppose you bought a cow, and took her home to milk her. As you pull up your stool and start milking her in anticipation of enjoying rich, wholesome milk, she pops you in the face with her tail. Then, like Balaam's donkey, she talks to you, much to your astonishment and chagrin.

"What do you think you are doing, big boy?"

"I-I'm m-milking you," you stammer. "I bought you, you belong to me, and now I am getting my milk!"

"Get your hands off me," she glowers ominously, "before I permanently separate your uppers from your lowers. You might have bought me, but that has nothing to do with my milk. I'll do with it as I see fit. It's *my* milk."

Incredible? Preposterous? Not at all. It is pretty much the modern concept of many young and old in reference to their "Christian" relationship to Christ. Bought by His blood for their salvation, but with the "milk" of their life, its talents, energy, purpose and decisions reserved for themselves. Scriptural? I doubt it.

Salvation involves turning from going one's own way (Isaiah 53:6), the very essence of sin, to Christ and going His way. It involves turning from being the self-centered god, boss, manager of one's own life to recognizing Christ as the new God, Boss, Manager, as well as one's Saviour from sin and Hell.

Luke 6:46 graphically illustrates this with the un-answerable question, "Why call ye me Lord, Lord and *do not* the things which I say?" To not obey is to clearly and ineluctably admit that Jesus is not one's Lord. Salvation is forever received by trusting Jesus Christ alone, not by works, as works neither save, help save, or keep one saved. Inevitably, however, in true salvation, good works flow from the new nature and from Christ dwelling within. Salvation must include believing on the LORD Jesus Christ.

Notice: Romans 10:9, "That if thou shalt confess with thy mouth the Lord Jesus, [Jesus as LORD], and shalt believe in thine heart that God hath raised him from the dead, thou shalt be—[what—dedicated? No!] SAVED."

What if a witch doctor you were witnessing to professed to accept Christ. You carefully laid the groundwork, explained who Jesus was and what salvation meant. Finally, the glorious day arrives when he says he fully understands, and he takes Jesus as his Lord and Saviour. You are overjoyed, but when you go back the next day, he is happily worshiping his gaudily-colored metal idol again, praying and bowing to it. Crestfallen, you again explain to him the gospel and who Jesus is, and what salvation consists of, and he reassures you that he fully understands, and that he has really accepted Jesus, and is very happy that he is now saved. Then he goes back to worshiping his idol! Weeks go by, then months, even years. The witch doctor attends Christian meetings, sings Christian songs, gives testimony, but continues to worship his idol and do its bidding as he interprets it. Would he really be a converted child of God? The answer both from Scripture and reason is obvious and he would not be.

By the same token, we must not delude ourselves that Jesus is our Lord and Saviour if we still insist on being the god, boss, manager of our life. To take Jesus as a fire escape from Hell, while still worshiping at the shrine of self, is tragically fatal to us, and to outreach for the lost in the name of Christ. Because true salvation and service are virtually inseparable, when we respond to the call for salvation, in seed form at least, we have also responded to the call for service. Remember, we do not serve in order to be saved, or to keep saved, but because we have been saved! As Livingston is reported to have said, "If Christ be God and died for me, then no sacrifice is too great to make for Him."

God's Plan for a Christian's Life

What *is* your purpose for life if you are truly converted to Jesus Christ? Who owns your life? Well, who bought it, and to whom did you give it? What does He want of it?

Jesus said, "From henceforth thou shalt catch men" (Luke 5:10b). Not just fish for them—catch them!

Where do you like to fish best? Where thousands of people are stepping all over each other with oftentimes the same bait in a lake known to have been heavily fished day after day for decades? Where fish are gorged with bait, and most of them swim wearily or disdainfully away as bait aplenty splashes near them from hordes of fishermen jockeying desperately for position and stumbling all over one another? Or would you prefer to fish where the terrain may be difficult, danger may lurk in the vicinity, the lake is attainable only after sacrifice and hardship, but oh, the hungry fish! Multitudes fight and starve for even one morsel of food, and many have never so much as seen one time the bait you have to offer.

If you prefer the latter fishing scene, that's missions!

One of the problems in determining one's life commitment is that the way of the cross looks so drear, and the way of Satan so enticing, filled with so many yummy goodies. The way of Satan is often disguised as the way of self, one's own intelligent, reasonable plan for one's life.

Mark this! If my plan and yours for our lives, however alluring and appealing it may seem, could succeed better than God's plan for our lives, then God would be a liar and a failure. In fact, He wouldn't be God anymore, which of course is impossible. If a creature can substitute a plan for his life better than the plan of the all-knowing God of the Universe, then he is smarter, wiser than God. God cannot let anyone's plan for his life succeed better than His plan, as this is a deliberate, rebellious challenge to His Godhood. Our plans, however well laid, will result in delusion and disaster, either or both here and hereafter. God's plan for our life, however outwardly unappealing, results in lasting peace, satisfaction, souls for Christ, and glory to Him.

It is true that God loves you and indeed does have a wonderful plan for your life. Part of that plan includes reaching others for Christ.

Jesus said, "For the Son of Man is come to seek and save that which was lost" (Luke 19:10). How clear! This was His purpose. He also said, "As my Father hath sent me, even so send I you" (John 20:21). Then, when we are saved, His purpose becomes our purpose, to seek and save the lost. In John 14:23, Jesus declared that if we loved Him we would do what He said, and beloved, this is the very heart of what He said.

Consider the following parable.

Imagine John, whose wife is on vacation, getting two old friends, Bob and Jack, to stay with his children while he goes out to get a haircut and incidentally to escape "kid-o-phobia." Sauntering out of the barber shop sometime later, he smells smoke. He sees his home in flames some four blocks away. He remembers that he left his children asleep upstairs and begins to run frantically toward home. Surely his trusted friends who have been left in charge of his precious children will have saved them from the fire.

As he approaches, to John's horror and consternation, he hears the screams of his children above the roar of the flames. He comes upon Bob and Jack casually leaning against a telephone pole, watching the house burn and listening to the children's piercing screams.

Bob says, "Hello, John. Look at your lawn. I noticed it needed mowing and I mowed it for you. Did a good job, too!"

Jack adds, "Look at your hedge. It was so ragged, and I clipped it for you. Sure hope you like it."

John cannot believe his ears. "Bob! Jack!" he cries, "what's wrong with you? My children are trapped and burning to death! Why, *why* didn't you save them?"

John runs to the house, but it is too late. Amid the last despairing screams of his children, the house collapses with a roar.

Brokenhearted, he stands there unable even to see the well-clipped hedge or the freshly mowed lawn through his blinding tears. His "friends" failed and his children are hopelessly, needlessly burned to death.

Histrionic, dramatic, overdrawn? Not if you really believe in Hell, and that people are going there. You see, this is a picture of those who could be God's children if we won them for Christ; otherwise they go to Hell to burn forever. Christ died for them, and He sends all Christians to win them, to rescue them from sin and Hell. How can we say we love Jesus or love souls if we, like Bob and Jack, put other things, even good things, first?

God wants us to be urgent about this harvest of souls. "Lift up your eyes, and look on the fields," Jesus said (John 4:35). Multitudes of Christians are showing God "lawns" they've mowed, "hedges" they've clipped for Him, while He weeps for souls. In the name of Jesus, commit yourself right now to winning souls to Him! There is a place, a wonderful place, for clipping hedges, mowing lawns for Him, but never in place of winning souls to Him.

Why should you make a life commitment? Jim Elliot, whose blood the Auca Indians shed on a lonely beach in Ecuador, answered this so succinctly: "He is no fool to give what he cannot keep, to gain what he cannot lose."

Sacrifice? Look at the cross! As Dr. Tom Malone once said, "I never gave up anything for Jesus. I just emptied my pockets of dirt, and He filled them with diamonds!"

There were times when my wife and I have gone hungry, when one of our sons was beaten, when a sick daughter in a cold miserable uninsulated log cabin in Alaska hovered between life and death, when men threatened to kill me. I am not talking about a life of chocolate bon bons, the gaining of this world's goods. Compared to many missionaries I know, our life has been on easy street. But when the first soul that found Jesus wept his way to the Saviour—that soul may otherwise have never heard—it was worth it all! And when Jesus says, "Well done, thou good and faithful servant," it will be worth it all a thousand times over!

The question is, when you look at the cross, when you see the lostness of men, particularly those who have had little chance or none, when you hear His command, "Go ye into all the world, and preach the gospel to every creature," and His love begins to work in your heart, do you really have any other honest choice than to commit yourself body and soul to wherever He leads?

Wherever God leads us, then, we should be sure of our decision, and use that place as a mission field for Him. It is just as legitimate to ask a lawyer or teacher or doctor how God called him into his profession as it is to ask a missionary how he was called into being a missionary.

Suppose a missionary answered such a question like this:

"Well, my daddy was one so I decided I would be too."

"I thought I could make more money doing this than anything else."

"A lot of my friends were doing it."

"I liked the prestige."

"I just kind of drifted into it."

"I liked to travel."

What would you think of him? Would you have much confidence in him as a God-called, God-led man? Shouldn't a Christian in any profession, then, have better answers than this?

It is also just as legitimate to ask a Christian lawyer, teacher, doctor, or whatever, what impact he is making on his world for Christ, who is coming to know Jesus and having their lives changed because of his ministry, as it is to ask a missionary the same questions.

Opportunities for Service for God

This brings us to the specific leading of God concerning

the opportunities for missionary service that are open today. Many mission groups now have a marvelous provision for Christians to serve as short-term missionaries or helpers, which is often a real help to career missionaries on the field.

It also helps prospective missionaries to decide (1) if they want to be a career missionary, (2) if God is calling them to that particular field. Both professionals, such as doctors, teachers, nurses, evangelists, counselors, bookkeepers, etc., and non-professionals are needed for terms of a year or two, or sometimes even for three to six months. Sometimes the work involves construction, helping out in Bible camps, Vacation Bible School, maintenance, helping nurses, and a myriad of tasks the missionary needs help in doing.

The short-termer has an opportunity to be of real and definite help to some of God's dedicated missionaries in the task that God has called them to do. His efforts, if performed in the unquestioning love of Jesus Christ, will be long remembered and greatly appreciated. He may prolong the ministry of an overworked, exhausted servant of God, or extend his outreach for souls for Christ. He will help meet needs both physical and spiritual, on the field to which he goes. He may bring much needed fellowship to barren places at times, and may encourage both the missionary and his children, if any. Though often limited by language on a short term, there remains the exciting possibility that both his enthusiasm and Christian love may result in either himself or the missionary leading people on the field to Jesus Christ.

If this were all, it would be more than enough, but there is much more. The short-termer will see missions deglamorized. He will eat food foreign to his taste. He will know the bite of loneliness. The utter frustration of the language barrier will grate on his nerves day and night.

So much to give and no way to give it!

He will know the humidity of an unbearable climate, or the aching cold of a hostile one, and wonder how people could ever stand to live there! He will fight to keep his quick and unwanted advice when he thinks he has a better way. He will encounter a culture in which things like time, so important to him, seem not to matter to those he has been sent to.

At times he may wonder why he is there and long desperately to be home, especially when his patience erodes away, his efforts seem unappreciated, and he has to fall to his knees in desperation before His Saviour. Dirt, so much of it; smells, how awful! Sin, how revolting! Surely there is no hope for these people. Sickness, disease, ugh. Oh, Lord, how I want to go home!

But then, the yearning need in soft brown eyes, the imploring hands, the need, the unutterable need! And finally, here and there, a little bit of harvest, a building built, a wound bound, a soul trusts Christ, and suddenly, this is "where it's at"! This is his reason for existence.

Or, he will face himself, and his Saviour, and say frankly, "This is not for me, at least, not here."

One young man came as a short-termer to Alaska one summer and shared with me in leading a dying young man in his twenties to Christ. He has since stated that this was the most meaningful experience of his life. For the first time he fully realized the desperate need of a soul, and his own need to be a soul winner. Oh yes, he helped in some carpentry work, and that too was very valuable to God, but his soul-winning experience was the essence of missions to him.

In determining God's will for you in going to a specific place of service, you may find the "Gospel Gun" to be very helpful. This gun has three sights, instead of the usual two, that must be lined up to ensure hitting the target, in this case, the center of God's will.

Sight one, James 1:5: "If any of you lack wisdom, let him ask of God, that giveth to all men liberally, and upbraideth not; and it shall be given him." Ask God for His wisdom which He has promised to give, and simply believe Him and thank Him for it.

Sight two, after gathering information pro and con, depending especially and most heavily on the Word of God, trusting that God is guiding your search, and your brain, make a decision, that you believe Jesus Himself would make under the circumstances. If the decision is from God, James 3:17 declares it will be pure, and especially peaceable. If you do not have peace about your decision, reassess the situation. There should be a sense of relief, of full committal at this point, obstacles or not, and increasing peace as time goes on, not a nagging uneasiness. This is particularly true at the times when you are nearest God and manifestly in His presence, though at other times Satan will mightily attack your decision.

Sight three, push on the door outwardly that is in accord with your inner decision, and God will open the door for you in due time. He will even overrule an honest mistake, as He did when He closed the door to Asia when Paul thought he should go there.

When you have these three sights properly lined up, squeeze the trigger of your life force and put all you've got into it. You are in God's will!

This test is God's seal of certainty to go, or reveals a closed door that says, "I want you elsewhere."

God help us to quit playing around interminably in the grays, and get to the black and white of life commitments for Jesus Christ, and for the souls of men.

CHAPTER 2

Frontiers for World Christians

Warren Webster

We live in a world where the sun never sets on the church of Jesus Christ. The fellowship of Christian believers is now more widely planted and more deeply rooted among more peoples than ever before in history.

"Even where there are no organized churches, even where missionaries are turned away with guns and Christianity is a forbidden faith, you will find Christians. Perhaps only one, two, a handful, perhaps only foreigners, but they are there, and they belong to the oldest and strongest worldwide fellowship the world has ever known, the people of God, the church of Jesus Christ," wrote Samuel Moffett, in his book, *Where'er the Sun.*

Accomplishments of the Past and Present

Contrary to popular assumptions, far more countries are open to the gospel today than are closed. No more than 17 of the 144 countries in the United Nations are closed or partially closed to missions. More than 90 per cent of the world's nations and territories are open to Christian proclamation—many of them more open than ever before. Even where doors are "closed" to outside missionaries you will generally find Christians already living and witnessing behind those doors. Moreover, through Christian radio and literature no country is completely closed to all Christian witness.

During more than 1900 years of history, Christianity has spread until it is now the largest and most widespread religious faith. More than 1 billion people would identify themselves as Christians. Unfortunately, there are far more professing Christians than "possessing" Christians. Nominal Christianity remains a massive problem pointing to the urgent necessity of re-evangelizing each new generation, especially in Western countries.

In the 185 years since William Carey went to India (1792 A.D.), marking the beginning of the modern missionary movement, the Christian faith has literally exploded around the world. During the past century and a half more people have become Christians and more churches have been planted than in the previous 1800 years of church history. In the past 60 years Protestants have multiplied 18 times in the non-Western world. Much of this growth has taken place in the last "twenty-five unbelievable years."

In Africa and Asia, where the Christian message is impacting non-Christians, the ratio of Christians to total population is rising rapidly. In Asia by 1900 there was only one Christian for every 75 non-Christians. Now there is one for every 22. In Africa in 1900 there was one Christian for every 28 non-Christians, but today there is one for every 2.5 Africans south of the Sahara.

In South America by 1900 there were only 50,000 Protestants. Today evangelical Protestants in Latin America number more than 20 million.

The great missionary fact of the twentieth century is that "the church is there . . ., the Body of Christ in every land, the great miracle of history, in which the living God himself through his Holy Spirit is pleased to dwell"

(Stephen Neill, in *A History of Christian Missions*).

Now that the church has become a worldwide reality the "home base" for missions is everywhere—wherever a church is found. All Christians are commanded to "go and tell." All Christians should be "World Christians." The task of missions is not simply a matter of crossing geographical and cultural frontiers, but also of evangelizing and discipling men and women on the frontier between faith in Christ and unbelief, wherever it exists. As such, the true missionary frontier—the conflict with paganism—runs through every land.

The Task Ahead

While a great deal has been accomplished in world evangelization and current progress is encouraging, there is much that remains to be done.

It is estimated that one third of the people on earth have never heard the Christian gospel in any form. At least another third have never had the claims of Christ presented to them in an intelligible way pointing toward personal decision and commitment to Christ.

Geographically, the Christian faith has achieved near universal dimensions with churches found on every continent and in nearly every nation. There are only one or two countries left, like the People's Republic of Mongolia in Asia, or Muslim Mauritania in West Africa, where there are no known believers. In a few places there may still be just a handful of believers, as in Afghanistan, Tibet, Libya and Albania which has proclaimed itself "the first atheist state." A recent study estimates that in Russia there is one believer for every 80 people, but in Turkey the estimated ratio of believers to total population is 1/800,000! These are frontiers that challenge "World

Christians."

Linguistically, some part of the Word of God has been translated into more than 1500 languages which are spoken by 97 per cent of the earth's people. This includes all major languages and is unquestionably the greatest achievement in translation communication which the world has ever known. But there remain some 4000 smaller languages and dialects spoken by 150 million people who don't yet have a single verse of Scripture available in their mother tongue. The vital task of New Testament translation for these peoples could be completed before the end of this century by dedicated "World Christians."

Even where Bibles or New Testaments are available in local languages, up to 90 percent of the people in some countries have never seen or owned a copy. There is a tremendous job of distribution yet to be done. In places like India, Pakistan and Bangladesh 70-80 per cent of the people could not read a Gospel portion given them in their mother tongue because of the high rate of illiteracy. These frontiers call for Christians in adult literacy education and in mass media that supplement or transcend the printed page.

Culturally, it has been estimated that 87 per cent of the world's people who do not profess the Christian faith are sealed behind cultural barriers that prevent them from being able to grasp the significance of the gospel for themselves. They are not presently "winable" by ordinary "near-neighbor" evangelism simply because they have no Christian neighbors, or none who understand their language or culture well enough to effectively communicate the gospel. At least 80 per cent of the non-Christians in the world today are culturally or geographically beyond the reach of existing churches. This means that "native missionaries using their own language" are not the easy solution some have imagined. The only way the unreached people will ever be effectively evangelized is for Christians somewhere to determine to cross the cultural barriers—of language, caste, tribe, social class and economic strata—in order to communicate the gospel in ways the unreached can comprehend.

A recent study indicates that 95 per cent of today's 40,000 Protestant missionaries (25,000 from North America) are focusing their efforts on communities that already claim to be Christian or on the 17 per cent of the world's non-Christian peoples who are in the immediate environment of existing churches. Only 5 per cent of the Protestant missionary force is majoring on the great unreached blocks of Muslims, Hindus and Chinese who comprise 83 per cent of the non-Christian world and number around 2 billion. These are major cultural frontiers which must be increasingly penetrated and permeated by "World Christians" concerned with world evangelization.

Contrasting Opportunities and Resources

The opportunities and resources for making Christ known vary widely from country to country. We live in a world of tremendous inequities and imbalance with respect to the distribution of the gospel message.

A recent Gallup Poll in the United States indicated that one in every three adult Americans surveyed claimed to have experienced the "new birth." Several studies have projected that there are 40-50 million evangelical Christians in the United States. By way of contrast there are only a few hundred believers among the 17 million people in Algeria (a ratio of 1/75,000). The estimated ratio of believers to total population in some other countries:

Afghanistan	1/500,000	Italy	1/500
Austria	1/1200	Libya	1/700,000
China	1/1000	Nepal	1/24,000
Iraq	1/19,000	Thailand	1/6000
Israel	1/35,000	Vietnam	1/700

It has been said that 90 per cent of the ordained ministers in the world work among the 9 per cent of the earth's people who speak English. A tremendous imbalance!

Dr. Don Hillis observes that no country in all of history has enjoyed as much "gospel surplus" as the U.S.A.:

There are 70 million Protestants in the U.S.A., and that is more than twice as many as in any other country in the world.

There are more people in Sunday school on any given Sunday in America than in all the rest of the world.

There are more young people in our Bible institutes and Bible colleges than in all the rest of the world.

There are more students in just one of our seminaries than in all the seminaries of Europe and Asia combined.

In just one of our Bible institutes, there are more students than in all such schools on the continent of Asia.

We have many times more hours of gospel broadcasting than any other nation.

There is more evangelical literature printed in English than in all the other languages of the world combined.

— From *I Don't Feel Called (Thank the Lord!)*.

Dr. Hillis also notes that no American is farther away from the gospel message than the turn of a radio or TV dial, and no further than a short drive to a church which is faithful in preaching the Good News. In comparison there are many countries where millions of people have no access to a gospel broadcast and have never been privileged to pass near a church that preaches the gospel. In view of this, he concludes: "To suggest that the United States is just as much a mission field as any other country is to promote a half-truth. If by that statement one means that an unsaved American is as unsaved as an unsaved Chinese, the statement is true. But if the statement implies that the remedy is as available to the Chinese as to the American, nothing could be farther from the truth. There are millions of people in the world to whom the message of God's saving grace is just not available in any form, and that is not true in the United States."

He further points out, "This does not mean that we as American believers can fold our hands and forget all about witnessing to our neighbors. Wherever God has placed us we are to be the light of the world—we are to be his witnesses. Recognizing this fact, however, it must be our determined purpose to get the gospel out to the millions who do not now have an opportunity to hear it. To proclaim the Good News to men and women in lands where it is not now available must be our priority." Though Americans make up only 1/17th of the world's population they have unequaled opportunity of access to the gospel—unless they choose to ignore it.

Americans also have proportionally greater resources for sharing the gospel than Christians do in most other places. Though comprising only 6 per cent of the world's people, the United States is using 40 per cent of world resources. Currently, 60 per cent of the manpower, and 80 per cent of the funding for Protestant missions comes from North America. Let us remember the words of Jesus who said, "To whom much is given, of him much will be required."

The challenge to be a "World Christian" applies to every believer and should last a lifetime. Any Christian can be one—from the youngest child to the oldest senior citizen. It has very little to do with where one lives or works. It simply involves "obedient availability" to . . .

Anything God wants you to do,
Any place He leads you to go,
Anything He needs you to give.

There will be those who go to other cultures, those who stay but are constantly and determinedly aware of world needs, and also those who stay but feel led and are chosen by their local church to give special, unusual emphasis to the vast world of need that is far from the eyes of the average American.

What kind of "World Christian" does God want you to be? Let us move forward across today's frontiers and make history, not just read about it!

CHAPTER 3

On Being a World Citizen

Charles Green

After serving as a missionary in Argentina for several years, I found it necessary, because of health problems, to return to the States where I am serving in a home mission program. This experience has taught me first of all that I am to be a missionary anywhere God puts me, and secondly, that although the adjustment to minister to another culture is greater overseas, the same qualities are called for here if I am to identify with and communicate with the people among whom I live. In other words, God wants me to declare His gospel as a "world citizen" no matter where I am.

God is certainly concerned where His servants are. Jesus commanded His disciples to "wait in Jerusalem." God asked discouraged and fearful Elijah hiding at Horeb, "What doest thou here?" Jonah's disobedient steps away from Nineveh were certainly observed by the Almighty. The Apostle Paul attempted to go to Bithynia but the "spirit allowed him not."

God does care where we are geographically, but He is even more concerned about what we are spiritually. Geography does not make the missionary; producing disciples does. As we move along in this life with its roadblocks, delays, detours and breakdowns, let's believe that we are exactly where God wants us and instead of being so concerned about geography, let's get concerned about serving the Lord here and now.

Reach Out!

First of all, let's reach out to others around us who need Christ. Are you aware of how small our circle of friends usually is? I'm not referring to acquaintances but to the people with whom we spend most of our time. Unless you are unusual, your really close friends number less than a dozen and more likely around a half-dozen. These friends mean a lot to you. When you are with them you feel secure, happy and comfortable—you belong. You never intended for this small group of friends to become a clique, but that's the way outsiders view it.

A small, inner circle of friends can form in your church, your neighborhood, or at school, and unless you take steps to break the clique barrier, it will imprison you and keep you from reaching others for Christ. Jonah didn't want to break out of his comfortable clique. He was willing to let the Ninevites perish because of his selfishness. The Apostle Paul presents an entirely different picture as he was willing to become all things to all men if by any means he could save some.

Who can you reach out to? To those who are also reaching out for help. Look for the new people, the lonely, the minority, the experience seekers. If your hands aren't stretched out offering friendship and Christian life, other hands will be extended which hold alcohol, drugs, and doctrines of false cults. In Acts 9:26,27, the Apostle Paul says that when he went to Jerusalem after his conversion the apostles were afraid to receive him but Barnabas took Paul and presented him to the inner circle. Barnabas reached out to Paul and the church has been grateful ever since.

If you are a young person, do you realize that the school

campus is one of the world's great mission fields? The 14,300,000 secondary school students in America represent more souls than found in such foreign fields as Jordan, Senegal, the Luzon Island of the Philippines, and the area of northern Argentina where I served put together!

You are where you live for a purpose. If you are a student, it is not by accident that God has put you in the school where you are. I was invited recently to give a series of lectures at our local high school. It was a great experience as I was impressed again by the intelligence, enthusiasm and vitality of youth. I left the campus burdened for the students' spiritual condition and wishing I could somehow enroll as a teenager to move among them and share the Good News of Jesus Christ. Obviously, I can't do that, but young people are already there as Christ's ambassadors to the high school campus. Let Him reach out through you—wherever you are.

Step Out!

Let's step out in obedience to the Great Commission. Too often our response to the missionary mandate is as if the starter had said, "On your mark, get set, RELAX!" We get a great vision of serving the Lord and winning souls, but that's the end of it. Jesus said, "GO." I believe that if the angels were permitted to talk to us they would form a great host of spectators pointing toward our doors and chanting, "Go, go, go!"

Our problem is one of inertia. "Inertia," as you remember from general science, is the property of matter by which it will remain at rest unless acted upon by some external force. We are kept inert by fear. The same fear that propels us toward the security of a small group of friends also restrains us from appearing to be a religious fanatic, odd, or different.

Recently, when calling from door to door in a neighborhood, my wife and I heard two men of Spanish origin speaking to each other in Spanish as they repaired a roof. They weren't aware that we could understand Spanish, so as we stopped at the house next to the one where they were working, we heard them say, "Here they come . . . they are some of those." They were quite surprised when we greeted them in their mother tongue and perhaps more than a little embarrassed.

Yes, we are "some of those," and the sooner we recognize it the better. The Christian is different. He is not of the world but rather is sent into the world to preach the Good News of salvation. He marches to a different drum. He strives to please a different master. And he knows that since he lives in an alien and hostile world, he will be the target of persecution. Whether in Africa, Hong Kong, Brazil, France, or the school campus, the Christian will stand out—sometimes because of his color and speech, but always because he is "of the Lord."

Doubt is another hindrance to our stepping out for Jesus. We wonder:

"Does the gospel have the power to transform a life?"

"How do I know Christianity is true?"

"Why are there so many different religions?"

"Who am I to be talking to others about the Lord? I've still got lots of faults myself."

Sound familiar? If so, you might be encouraged to know that every Christian worker has suffered similar attacks of doubt. Paul knew this would happen and therefore wrote, "Above all, taking the shield of faith, wherewith ye shall be able to quench all the fiery darts of the wicked" (Ephesians 6:16).

When the Lord Jesus said, "Follow me, and I will make you fishers of men" (Matthew 4:19), He knew that each step would be a step of faith. I believe the greatest remedy for doubt is to counterattack with faith. As a young man of 21, I was preparing a sermon for my home church in Arizona as they intended to license me to preach the gospel in a special service. While preparing the message, every doubt conceivable plagued me. Toward the end of the afternoon I still had nothing written for the sermon. Satan had defeated me with doubts.

I realized this and decided to counterattack. Taking my Bible and tracts I went to a camp for cotton harvesters on our farm and began going from door to door witnessing to God's grace and goodness. After an hour, I returned victoriously, full of faith and love for God. The message came quickly and easily and I had no trouble delivering it with conviction.

"It works!" was my reaction after leading my first soul to Christ in Latin America. The gospel that saves people in North America has the same power to transform lives anywhere in the world. I knew that in my mind but the actual experience of the truth thrilled my heart.

Still another reason for inertia which keeps us from stepping out for Christ is laziness. Can Christians be lazy? Can young people be lazy? That is like asking if a frog can hop. Sure, young people can be lazy, and pastors and missionaries and deacons and all the other Christians can be lazy. But that doesn't excuse laziness in us. Jesus said to the man who buried his talent, "You wicked and lazy servant."

God gives those of us who have problems with laziness a striking teaching example in Scripture. He doesn't use the example of some rich industrialist. In fact, He doesn't use an example of a man at all. He directs our attention down—and farther down—to the tiny, almost unnoticed ant and says, "You can learn some great lessons from this insect which has no guide, overseer or ruler and yet works all summer long to prepare for winter" (see Proverbs 6:6-8).

Enough for the reasons for inertia. Let's release the emergency brake and get our service for the Lord in gear.

Stepping out for Christ begins at one's doorstep. It sounds so exciting to go to historical Europe, colorful Argentina, or the exotic Philippines, but missionary work begins at home. In Acts 1:8 Jesus said, ". . . And ye shall be witnesses unto me both in Jerusalem, and in all Judea, and in Samaria, and unto the uttermost part of the earth." Even though we would like to hop, skip and jump over that principle, it remains valid. The road to "uttermost city" begins at your home town.

If you have a special gift for reaching across cultures, there are probably abundant opportunities to do that near you. I live in Farmington, New Mexico, on the edge of the Navajo Indian reservation. More than one half of the people in our county are Navajo. My Jerusalem, therefore, includes many people of a language and culture different from mine. My son Randy, attending a college in Denver, assists in a Spanish-speaking church. He tries to bring people to the Lord and to the church from a variety of backgrounds, all the way from Mexican, Cuban and Puerto Rican kids in the inner city to Venezuelan engineering students studying at the School of Mines in Golden, Colorado.

What other cultures are represented in your home town? African, Latin American, Chinese, Vietnamese? In 1975 approximately 400,000 people were legally admitted to our country. So, the world comes to us and that is a good deal easier than our going to the world—or is it? The first step out of our doorway, whether to witness across the street or across the world, is the most difficult.

Within a short distance from your front door very likely there are hospitals, rest homes, jails, homes for juvenile delinquents and ghettos, all needing the gospel as much as your neighbors. Will you step out for Jesus? Faithful steps now, even though they are small and few, will lead to greater distances and opportunities in the years ahead.

Speak Out!

In the third place we need to learn to speak out for our Lord. At times in the course of modern missions it has been expressed that the presence of a dedicated Christian was all that was needed on the mission field—the good life would speak for itself. A righteous life is essential, but the concept of a silent witness falls far short of the scriptural principle. Jesus said, "preach," "teach," "tell." He could not have meant that the presence of a dedicated Christian in the midst of non-Christians was sufficient. He certainly was saying, "Speak out!"

The Apostle Paul preached, warned, and taught publicly and from house to house. He wrote to his young disciple to "preach the word," and said of himself, "Woe is unto me, if I preach not the gospel!" Faith, he said, "comes by hearing, and hearing by the Word of God." And, "How shall they hear without a preacher?"

Agreed, we must speak as well as be. Then how should one speak out?

First we need the weapon of God's Word in our arsenal. God promised to use His Word as a sword or as a fire or as a hammer. All three metaphors fit the idea of a spiritual confrontation. Memorization of scriptures is the best way to have God's Word ready for instant use. You may desire to use the Navigator's Bible Memory System or develop one of your own. The important thing is to hide the Word in your heart.

Along with committing Bible verses to memory, a person needs to learn how to use the Word, to know which passages and verses are appropriate for certain arguments and doubts. He needs to have in his mind key verses which he can readily use to introduce a person to Christ. In fact, it would be well to be able to lead a soul to the Lord with verses from one book of the Bible, such as Romans or John. Marking those verses in the other person's Bible will enable him to review the plan of salvation when alone.

God's message deserves a positive and convincing presentation. The Christian faith has nothing for which to apologize. The gospel is called the "Gospel of God," a "glorious gospel," and Paul says it is the "power of God unto salvation." We need not be ashamed of it!

The offense of the cross refers to the biting, convicting truth that all are sinners and can come to God only through faith in Christ. That offense cannot be lessened nor should we want to lessen it. We must be careful, however, that we do not add to it a personal offense of tactlessness, rudeness or pride. "Shun profane and vain babblings," Paul instructs Timothy. I knew an old English missionary who went from house to house in a town of northern Argentina calling the people away from their household tasks and relaxation to tell them, "You are going to hell." Her rude and abrupt announcement awakened no sense of repentance in her hearers but rather anger. Thus the life-giving message was obscured by a personal offense. Speaking out for Christ deserves a positive, courteous and tactful approach.

In addition to speaking out positively, our witness for Jesus Christ needs to be personal. If one is saved and living for Christ, the Holy Spirit has given him a "shine." In Philippians, chapter 2, verse 15, the child of God is described as living in the midst of a crooked and perverse nation, among whom he shines as a light in the world. Jesus tells us in Matthew 5:16 that we should let our light shine before men. This shining is not anything we try to do, but rather what the Holy Spirit does in and through us as we are yielded to Him.

Our opportunity comes, however, when we are asked to explain the shine. Why do we not become angry and vengeful when wronged? Why do we care for the poor? Why do we not discriminate against those of other races? Or why do we spend so much time in the church? Why do we look so happy? Nothing you can say apart from the Word of God is more effective than your personal testimony, which if real and in agreement with God's revealed truth, is absolutely irrefutable. Use your personal testimony freely. It is uniquely yours.

With Resurrection Power

Now that we have discussed reaching out, stepping out and speaking out for Christ, let's turn our attention to the power source for all of this. During the gas shortage cars lined up for blocks to purchase precious petrol. Some even added auxiliary tanks to their vehicles. Why? The answer is simple: no gas, no go. Likewise, we mustn't forget the "filling station" for resurrection power. Significantly, the greatest of all missionary accounts (the book of Acts) begins with waiting. Chapter 1 reveals the disciples waiting ten days for the promise of the Holy Spirit. Why the long wait? Wasn't that wasted time? Doesn't the work of the gospel require haste? The reason for the waiting was to impress upon the disciples the need to depend upon God.

Without the Holy Spirit these early believers were not equipped for the gigantic task awaiting them. They needed the Holy Spirit for wisdom and guidance but most of all for power. "But ye shall receive power, after that the Holy Ghost is come upon you; and ye shall be witnesses . . ." (Acts 1:8). All the books in the world on church growth or missionary methods cannot take the place of the Holy Spirit. The third Person of the Godhead gives wisdom, utterance, boldness, joy and comfort to the Christian and uses the Word of God and the testimony of the believer to convict the world of sin and the need to be saved.

Everything I have mentioned as being important, whether we live at home or abroad, is completely impossible to achieve without power from above. Jesus said, "Without me you can do nothing." How imperative it is, then, to *reach out, step out* and *speak out* in the power that God gives rather than in the energy of the flesh. The command to go and make disciples of all nations is based on the fact that "all power" belongs to Christ who sends us forth.

The Apostle Paul states in Philippians, chapter 2, that all those things that really mattered to him before he became a Christian suddenly lost their value. In fact, he relegates his previous status symbols to the garbage dump. What Paul desires now is to know more of Christ and His resurrection power (Philippians 3:10). That power gives victory over sin as easily as it gave new life to a dead corpse; that power enables one to die to selfish desires just as Christ willingly gave up His life; that power brings victory out of seeming defeat even as the Lord, by dying, destroyed him that had power over death, the devil.

In our day of rapid change and transition when career missionaries come and go with greater ease, when other missionary personnel go to the field for a specified time only, when political conditions and the development of the national church affect the placement of missionaries, when the moral condition of America approximates that of "heathen lands," it becomes necessary that all of us seek to be missionaries at large—serving Christ wherever He leads us.

In July of 1972 my family and I were on our way back to Argentina. We were endeavoring to return by land to learn as much as possible about the Latin American people and their culture. I was hospitalized in San Jose,

Costa Rica, where we had spent a year in language study ten years earlier. Not responding to treatment I was flown to Miami, Florida, where my illness was diagnosed as viral meningitis. I didn't understand the Lord's doings but neither did I question His perfect will. I was able to lead a fellow patient and a student nurse to the Lord.

When I felt sufficiently strong we continued to Argentina where God gave me two more fruitful years in the church planting ministry. Recurring symptoms of dizziness, insomnia and neuritis made it seem advisable to return to the States for further testing and rest. That is when God led to our present ministry where He is confirming His call.

The point of this brief testimony is that Christ's resurrection power extends not only over sin and self but over circumstances. The Apostle Paul wrote his most joyful epistle, the letter to the Philippians, from a Roman prison. When he asked for deliverance from a thorn in the flesh, Christ's answer was, "My grace is sufficient for thee: for my strength is made perfect in weakness." Paul's response was, "Most gladly, therefore, will I rather glory in my infirmities, that the power of Christ may rest upon me."

I see the mission field as the world, and His laborers as all those committed to doing His will. Let's join in the task of reaching out, stepping out and speaking out wherever we are . . . and don't forget to look up for resurrection power.

CHAPTER 4

The Basis
for Missions

Bruce Ker

The scope of missions is very large, and significantly growing. Tens of thousands of individuals are involved in the proclamation of the gospel of Jesus Christ and the growth and the development of His church around the world. Not all of these individuals come from North America and wear white skins. An increasing number of God's missionaries are wearing black, brown, yellow and red skins, and are supported by vigorously growing churches in the third world nations.

This term, "third world," refers to newly independent and developing nations around the world. These churches are maturing and recognizing that the Biblical implications for missions need to be faced and fulfilled by their churches. So we have Indonesian missionaries working for the Lord Jesus in India. We have Korean missionaries proclaiming the gospel and building His church in Thailand. And the list of examples is long!

In addition to the increasingly large company of people directly involved in the exciting ministry of missions, the total budget for world missions has reached staggering proportions. Recently one church in North America has exceeded the million dollar mark in its missionary budget! In a day of rampant inflation it is taking considerably more dollars to support the work of missions. In the years to come the financial involvement in missions is undoubtedly going to continue to grow and expand.

This growth and development in missions must be placed in the context of the growth and development of the population of the world. The scope of the problems of feeding, housing, educating and caring for all of the needs of an exploding world population is simply staggering! The rate of growth, not only of the population of our world, but also in the overwhelming dimensions of world needs, must be considered carefully in terms of the mission of the church of Jesus Christ. It can readily be seen the vast importance and magnitude of the subject of missions.

The shaggy, stereotyped concepts which many people still carry concerning missions must be changed. Christians should not allow pessimistic thoughts regarding missions to linger in their minds. As we keep looking unto our Lord Jesus Christ we should remind ourselves that as members of His team we are on the victorious side. His purposes will certainly be accomplished in this world.

We also need to be "tuned in" to the new era and the present circumstances in missions.

The old image is that of a missionary possessed of the mediocre, wallflower-type personality trudging along a jungle path in a khaki uniform with a thick sun helmet on his head, a rifle grasped in one hand and a Bible in the other. Wild animals are lurking in the jungles beside the path. Naked savages, even hungry cannibals, are hiding in the shadows. The pagans are living in total poverty, covered with putrid ulcers, and living in fear of wild witch doctors. Their children are runny-nosed and pot-bellied and completely naked.

This is not the picture today. We must realize that the world situation has changed so much that in very few parts of the world do such situations exist. So the stereotyped images must be buried. We must realize that the winds of change have been blowing in all parts of the world, creating new situations.

The message of missions and the need for missions, however, has not changed. The message of redemption is still of first importance. God's love for lost men remains impelling, strong, and eternal. Men still come to a saving life-changing knowledge of Jesus Christ in the same basic way as they have through the centuries.

God's purpose in this world of men remains the same. This world of apparent chaos, disorder, and evil cannot change or hinder God's great eternal purpose and design. At the pivot point of God's purpose is His Son, our Lord Jesus Christ, and His redeeming work. He desires all men to become related to Himself through the Person, and as a result of the work of the Lord Jesus Christ. No force on earth or in hell can frustrate that purpose.

The implementation of this great, grand, and glorious purpose is to be through the body of Jesus Christ, called the church. As the physical head and physical body are vitally, intimately, and significantly related, so Jesus Christ is related to His church. It is through this spiritual relationship that the significant purposes of God in this world are accomplished.

The Character of Missions

Much missionary effort and interest falls short of being scripturally satisfactory because of an inadequate understanding of the missionary enterprise. Many Christians' minds have not interacted with the clear teaching of Scripture, but instead their emotions have led them into faulty thinking concerning missions. Merely romantic ideas or the stirrings of pity are inadequate conceptions of missions. A solid understanding of the true character of missions as revealed in the textbook of

Scripture is necessary.

The missionary movement did not start in the brain or heart of men like William Carey, Adoniram Judson, Hudson Taylor, nor even of the great Apostle Paul. So we ask the question:

Where does missions start? Where do we look for the actual starting point of the great missionary movement? If we find where missions really starts we probably can learn something about its true character.

1. Does missions start with the Great Commission? This is the usual response. But often the implications of the Great Commission in its textual setting is misunderstood. Later in this chapter we will attempt to throw some light on the Great Commission texts.

But if we designate the Great Commission passages, where the New Testament writers quote the words of our Lord Jesus Christ, as the starting point of missions, then there is the great problem and dilemma of what to do with the teaching of the Old Testament. The Old Testament is somewhat useless, if missions starts with the Great Commission passages. We have to look back before the utterance of the Great Commission of our Lord Jesus Christ for the beginning point of missions.

2. Does missions start with the great incarnation event? The incarnation was when God became flesh and Jesus Christ was born in Bethlehem. Certainly this was an event of great significance. Many people feel that in the life of Jesus Christ we find the starting point of missions. But really, the beginning point of missions is even beyond the great incarnation event.

3. Does missions start with the Old Testament records? There is definitely a missionary purpose and message in the activities in the Old Testament record. Many of the Old Testament prophets had a missionary thrust in their ministry. The work of the prophet Jonah proclaiming the

message of God to the Ninevites is a notable illustration of this. There is much of the missionary motif in the life and ministry of Abraham who was called out from his kindred to serve God among another people. Even in the Biblical account of Adam there are elements of missions apparent.

But notice carefully that if we can pinpoint the beginning of missions with man, then missions necessarily becomes man-made, and to that degree humanistic. So where does missions start?

4. Did missions start in eternity with God? YES, IT DID! The Bible reveals that missions is the very heart and character of God Himself. His nature makes missions inevitable. This means that missions is no afterthought or a matter of secondary consideration with God. It is of utmost importance. There are two aspects of the nature of God which are of prime significance as we consider the beginning point of missions.

• His Holiness. This characteristic of the nature of God indicated the tremendous need for missions, as well as the possibility of missions. Because God is so infinitely holy He alone could devise a way for establishing fellowship and relationship with mankind who are inherently, characteristically unholy. And He did so. The Bible reveals that God's holiness is a very basic attribute of His nature. This holiness has an activity to it which you will readily see is an essential characteristic for missions. The whole plan of missions is a very natural outcome of a holy God.

• His Love. If the holiness of God indicates the need and possibility of missions, then this characteristic of God's nature—His love—provides the basis and power for missions. God's great love is active and outgoing. There is a reaching out by God toward man. Completely understanding the spiritual need of man, God bends every effort to meet that need. In no other religious system is this great drama so beautifully portrayed as in scriptural revelation.

Here is where missions truly begins—in the very heart of God. God who made the world, not only in its physical dimension, but also in its human dimension, has a deep and eternal interest and concern for His world. It is continually on His heart.

In John 1:1 we read, "In the beginning was the Word." Verse 14 indicates that this is a reference to God's Son, the Lord Jesus Christ, who became flesh and lived among us. "The Word" speaks of communication. And missions is the communication of God's message to His world. The beginning point of this program was in eternity in the very heart and mind of our God.

There is the answer to the first question. Now the second question which we need to discuss is:

What does missions mean? We will receive help and understanding of what missions is all about by approaching the question in the following three ways.

1. Etymologically. This is a branch of the science of linguistics which is concerned with the formation and meaning of words themselves. Our English word, "mission," comes from the Latin word, *missio*. This Latin word means "a sending."

The word "mission" does not actually appear in our New Testament in the English language, but its idea is certainly present. The New Testament apostles were "sent ones," from the root meaning of the Greek word. The church at Jerusalem sent out Peter and Barnabas on specific missions. The church at Antioch later sent out Barnabas and Saul on what we call "the first missionary journey." There are therefore the ideas of (1) an authoritative sending forth, (2) the conveying of an important message by a designated messenger, (3) the recipients and auditors of that message and messenger, and (4) the accountability and relationship of the messenger to the individual or body sending him and his message. The study of the Word helps us understand the meaning of missions.

2. Biblically. The Bible is a missionary book throughout. This is true not because it contains isolated texts with a missionary flavor, but because the main line of argument that binds all of it together is the unfolding and gradual execution of a missionary purpose. The Bible is the story of the redeeming God entering the life-stream of the human race and creating a special people who would be the messengers of His redeeming grace to a needy world. In the Old Testament era this was accomplished through His chosen race Israel. In the New Testament era the agent for accomplishing this purpose is His body, the church. God is glorified when multitudes of men come to a transforming knowledge of Himself. Thus missions comprises both the warp and the woof of Biblical tapestry throughout.

3. Theologically. It helps to understand the meaning of missions when we see that the supreme desire of God is to reconcile all things to Himself. In this He is glorified. The great sovereign working of God's grace throughout eternity makes us believe in the reality of missions. It is by God's grace that a company of redeemed humanity is called out of sin and darkness unto Himself. Men and women become spiritually incorporated into a living body of which Christ is the head. This is His glorious church throughout the world—a many-splendored thing. Every single aspect and department of theology takes on significant meaning and clarity in terms of missions.

Summary: The character of missions is both great and glorious. It is such because it is rooted and founded in the very character of God—His holiness and His love. Because His great love overflows and reaches out, we have missions. Let us constantly possess this great view of missions. Can you find yourself in this glorious program of world missions?

The Foundation of Missions

Let us now briefly consider selected aspects of the Biblical and theological foundation of missions.

Biblical foundation of missions. Because Jesus Christ is the head of the church and gave to His apostles, who are the foundation men of the church, certain directives, we do need to study the Great Commission of Jesus Christ. These thoughts are also important because they are among the final words which Jesus uttered on earth before returning to His present position at the right hand of the throne of God in heaven. We will first list the references where the Great Commission is found, and then briefly discuss two of these. Here are the references:

(1) Matthew 28:16-20
(2) Mark 16:15,16
(3) Luke 24:44-49
(4) John 20:19-23
(5) Acts 1:6-8

Please realize that it is a combination of all five references that gives us a true picture of what the Great Commission is all about. Each passage makes its own unique contribution and is therefore significant. Not all of these utterances were spoken by our Lord Jesus on the same occasion. But they were spoken by Him at the same period of His life, after His resurrection from the dead and prior to His ascension to heaven.

Note the main emphases in these five passages. Matthew emphasizes the ministry of making disciples.

Both Mark and Luke emphasize the preaching and proclaiming of the gospel of Jesus Christ. John emphasizes the pattern or example of Jesus Christ as the sent one of God. Luke, in his account in Acts, emphasizes the power for worldwide witness.

It should be noted that the entire book of Acts gives us the unfolding of the model of apostolic missions. This record is rich in missionary principles and methodology.

It should also be noted that the epistles of Paul are directed to groups of people or specific individuals involved in his own ministry of missions. Paul was a great missionary statesman and his epistles contain great help for modern-day missionaries and their methodology.

Certain aspects of Matthew's account need to be stressed. Matthew indicates that when the eleven disciples recognized their Lord on that Galilean mountaintop, they came to Him, fell at His feet, and worshiped Him (Matthew 28:16,17). By this act they humbly submitted to His lordship. Then you will notice that the first phrase that came from our Lord's lips was a tremendous declaration of sovereign authority. He claimed that all authorities both on earth and in heaven were His (verse 18).

It is essential for all of us in missions to recognize this fact. We must do as the disciples did and humble ourselves in worship at His feet. We must accept His authority. If we truly recognize His authority in our lives we will not become frustrated in the ministry of missions. For example, considerations of geography will have secondary importance if we fully recognize the authority of Jesus Christ in missions. The Lord of missions possesses worldwide sovereignty! He is our Lord. And He is the responsible One in missions. We simply serve Him.

What is the main verb spoken by Jesus in this paragraph? It is not the word "go." It is "make disciples."

It is important that God's followers be ready to move out with Him, or to go forward. Jesus had this attitude of readiness. The ministry of missions is a dynamic one, never static. There is continual growth and movement in missions. We cannot afford the luxury of standing still in our attitudes of missions ministry. But the main thrust of His words is on the ministry of disciple-making. He describes this ministry with the two participles, "baptizing" and "teaching." So Jesus Christ was sending out His disciples in order for them to reproduce themselves by making other disciples. Let us look more closely at these two words.

1. Baptizing. This participle comes from the verb that means "to dip." The usage indicates the act of placing someone or something in close relationship with another object or person. For example, in I Corinthians 10:2 we read that the nation Israel was baptized unto Moses in the cloud and in the sea. In escaping from Egypt, the Israelites chose a close relationship with their leader, Moses. Baptism is used to indicate an initiation or an identification process. Disciples, then, are those individuals who choose to become identified with Jesus Christ. This suggests evangelism. So in the process of the ministry of missions disciples are made first by any and all forms of evangelism. This is the way people learn to become identified with Jesus Christ. They take on a new identity, or a new relationship.

2. Teaching. Our Lord spoke this participle, which further describes the ministry of disciple-making. Teaching is not a proclamation of the gospel, nor the announcing of the Good News, but something more. It is instruction in the Christian life. Disciples are learners. In order to have learning there needs to be instruction. They are to be taught to keep all the things which Jesus had commanded them. The things which the eleven disciples

had learned from Jesus were to be passed on to others (see II Timothy 2:2).

The first participle, baptizing, really indicates the glorious ministry of birth. The second, the teaching participle, points to the essential ministry of growth. So the ministry of disciple-making can be summed up as birth and growth. And this is what missions is all about.

This task no doubt appeared tremendously awesome to the eleven. Jesus, in the closing phrase, relieves their fear and timidity by promising them His presence continually. All of this, of course, is a tremendous incentive for missions. As we remind ourselves of His presence with us continually the task becomes easy and light. All things truly are possible when Jesus is with us.

In Acts 1:8 we have another key part of the ministry of missions. Jesus promises His disciples that they will receive power when the Holy Spirit comes upon them. This coming upon them with power happened at the occasion of Pentecost, as recorded in Acts 2. He also indicated that they would be witnesses of Him both in Jerusalem and in all Judea and Samaria and unto the uttermost part of the earth. This action is not in sequence, nor is it alternative. They in their day and we in ours do not have the alternative choice of being His witnesses wherever we please. Nor are we to stay in our Jerusalem until it is completely evangelized, and then move on to the next area. The "both" and "and" indicate that the action is to be simultaneous. While the witnessing is going on in Jerusalem it should also be going on in these other places. This gives us the broad Biblical dimension for missions as to its area of activity.

Theological foundation of missions. We have already pointed out the Biblical basis for missions. From the scriptural sources there are certain obvious theological assumptions.

First, God is absolutely sovereign. This means that He does not have to answer to any other being in the universe. He is completely sufficient unto Himself. This takes into account His complete wisdom as well as His complete love and holiness. All of God's actions and activities must be considered in the light of the sovereign greatness of our living eternal God. We have to realize continually that this sovereign God is in complete control of His Universe, down to every detail. He is working all things according to His infinite and wise plan and purpose.

Secondly, we have to realize that the Scripture reveals that human nature is exceedingly sinful and therefore under the just condemnation of God who is infinitely holy. Romans 3 gives us ample evidence of this dreadful fact. The earlier chapters in Romans reveal the fact that mankind has rejected the grace of God. As a result of man's rejection of God he stands under God's righteous judgment.

Thirdly, we stand back and marvel as we read in Scripture the description of God's infinite grace. Because of our sinfulness every one of us stands condemned justly before God. But because of God's grace those who trust in His Son as Saviour receive forgiveness and pardon for sin and an inheritance that is eternal. We deserve nothing from the Lord. If He did nothing for any of us He would still be a just God. But because of His amazing grace there are saved human beings.

Fourthly, we realize with thanksgiving that God provides His saved ones with spiritual power to live lives that are pleasing to Him, and are satisfying to us. This power, of course, is a reference to the indwelling Holy Spirit. Not only does the Holy Spirit regenerate the sinner, but He unites that sinner with others in fellowship and relationship of the body of Christ.

Fifthly, it is foundationally important to realize that

this activity of God the Holy Spirit is taking place around the world in many nations and cultures. God is calling out a people for Himself. This is the church, in its broadest dimensions. Local congregations are springing up all over the world at an accelerating rate. In some nations the rate of growth of the church of Jesus Christ far exceeds the rate of growth of the population of the country. And as noted earlier, these newly developing churches are catching the vision of missions and sending out their own disciple-makers, to proclaim the gospel, teach believers and plant new congregations.

Summary. Missions is a dynamic and glorious movement of God's grace. It finds its beginning point in the very heart and nature of God Himself in eternity past. The missionary movement is in a real way the extension of the love of God, throbbing, moving and motivating His children to carry His message of love to all people. Missions has a solid Biblical basis both in the Old Testament, and then more fully developed in the New Testament record. The local church, as the visible, tangible manifestation to the world of the body of Christ, is God's responsible agent for missions. The mission of the church is missions, and the mission of missions is the church.

CHAPTER 5

The Model for Missions

Bruce Ker

In the pages of the New Testament record we have an excellent model for missionary activity. Both in the example of our Lord Jesus Christ and in the pattern of His early followers we have excellent guidelines for our missionary enterprise in this generation. We recall the record of Matthew 16:18 where Jesus declares His purpose to build His church, even in the face of hellish opposition and authority. We have already seen that Christ possesses cosmic authority and power; that His purpose and plan is absolutely sovereign. The New Testament record gives us a marvelous account of the outworking of this church building plan to our Lord Jesus Christ.

The Method of Missions

As we consider the method of missions there are four matters which need to occupy our attention and which are clearly visible in the missionary record of the New Testament. Remembering that the overall purpose of God is to glorify His Son as the head of the church we will see that (1) Christ is the founder of the church, (2) the Holy Spirit is the power for the building of the church, (3) the church itself is its own agent of growth and development, and (4) history is the record of this dynamic method.

Christ the Founder. In the fullness of time God sent forth His Son (Galatians 4:4). Here we see God's significant movement from the nation Israel, which failed, to the individual Jesus Christ, who founded the worldwide movement, to God. Israel as a nation had been designated a kingdom of priests. The blessings of God were to spread to all Gentile nations through His selected nation, Israel. But the Israelites cherished the blessings of the Almighty strictly unto themselves. They entertained racial prejudice and cultural self-centeredness. From that very nation God raised up an individual, His own Son Jesus Christ, sent from heaven above. Jesus was the foundation stone of the great building program of God Almighty.

According to the prophecy of Zacharias, Jesus Christ would give light to those sitting in darkness and in the shadow of death (Luke 1:76-79). The angels appearing to the shepherds brought good news of great joy to *all the peoples* (Luke 2:9-14). The testimony of Simeon in that same chapter is also significant: "For mine eyes have seen thy salvation, which thou hast prepared before the face *of all people;* a light to lighten the Gentiles, and the glory of thy people Israel" (Luke 2:30-32). By these significant and spectacular announcements Jesus Christ was designated as the initiator, or founder of a significant movement.

There is also a specific pattern seen in the life of Jesus Christ, the founder of missions. This pattern gives us the basic methodology for each of our Lord's disciples in every succeeding period of church history. The Son of God moved in three spheres of life and ministry.

1. In Relationship to His Father. As you read the Gospel accounts you are aware of the continual need our Lord manifested for fellowship with His Father. We find repeated references to our Lord's prayer life. As Jesus Christ maintained a vital intimate relationship with God

His Father, so must we, each of His disciples, in fulfilling His ministry here on earth.

2. In Relationship to His Disciples. These disciples were men Jesus chose with care. They did not come from among the religious leaders of that day. They were ordinary men, chosen from ordinary walks of life. In Mark 3:14 we find His purpose in choosing them. They were to be with Him, and to be sent out to preach. The role of the disciples then was to listen to Him, to watch, to cooperate, and to receive training on the job. Jesus Christ trained them to reach out to others, and thus to establish a chain of ministry (II Timothy 2:2). This is a significant pattern for the ministry of missions provided by our Lord and His followers, and to be duplicated by us His followers today.

3. In Relationship to the Multitudes. When Jesus saw the crowds in Galilee or Judea, He was moved with compassion repeatedly. We see here the manifestation of His tender heart. So we deduce that the world mission of the church must be carried on in this pattern of the founder of the church. He maintained close fellowship with the Father, while involved in the training ministry of His disciples to reach out to needy peoples, and with tender-hearted compassion for the multitudes in His world. May God give us grace to carefully follow the pattern of Christ our founder.

There is also a splendid principle, among many possible principles, which needs to be noted as we consider Christ the founder of missions. This principle could be reduced to one word, "mobility." This also is exemplified in the life of the Son of God. He did not allow Himself to put down roots anywhere. Jesus showed a continuous effort to reach out. Without denying the deep needs of Capernaum, we see in Luke 4:43 that Jesus said, "I must preach the good news of the Kingdom of God to other cities also: for therefore am I sent." So we see Jesus constantly pressing on.

In John 10:16 we hear Him saying, "I have other sheep that are not of this fold: them also I must bring, and shall hear my voice; and there shall be one fold, and one shepherd." So Jesus Christ was mobile. He developed a strategy with His early disciples that was keyed to this principle of mobility. It would do well for all of us to ponder this aspect of the example of the founder of missions.

From Christ the founder of missions, we turn now to: *The Holy Spirit the Energizer.* The Lord Jesus, before He went back to heaven, promised His followers the gift of the Holy Spirit. This indwelling person of the Holy Trinity is surely the great enabler of missions. Let us consider the Holy Spirit's four-fold relationship.

1. Relating to the Great Commission. In every New Testament passage where the Great Commission is found recorded, there is either a direct or indirect reference to the blessed Holy Spirit. Notice also that whereas the Great Commission was spoken by our Lord Jesus before His return to heaven, the implementation of it awaited the internalizing effect of Pentecost. So there was no missionary activity until after Pentecost and the birth of the church. Pentecost, and the coming of the Spirit of God on man, made the church a witnessing church. The Holy Spirit is the great energizer or the great enabler who makes possible the carrying out of the Great Commission.

2. Relating to the Apostles. Right after the events of the closing days of our Lord's life here on earth the apostles were in great need of power. They had experienced tremendous stress surrounding the rejection and crucifixion of their Lord Jesus. They needed power in view of the extent of the task which Jesus left with them. They also needed power in view of the limits of their own

physical strength. They also needed power in view of the blessed promise of the Lord, "Behold I am with you always, even unto the end of the age." And so we find the gift of the Holy Spirit described in significant and powerful terms in Acts 2:1-4, "When the day of Pentecost was fully come, they were all with one accord in one place. And suddenly there came a sound from heaven as of a rushing mighty wind, and it filled all the house where they were sitting. And there appeared unto them cloven tongues like as of fire, and it sat upon each of them. And they were all filled with the Holy Ghost, and began to speak with other tongues, as the Spirit gave them utterance." There were obvious and rather immediate results from the gift of the Holy Spirit in power. Not only were they free to speak out the message of the Lord, but there was remarkable effectiveness as a result of their ministry (Acts 2:5-7,41,47). They were also made courageous even in the face of persecution as a result of the Holy Spirit's power in them (Acts 4:13,20,31). In short, the powerful presence of the Holy Spirit in the apostles made transformed men out of them.

3. Relating to the Church. According to Romans 8:9 every person receiving Jesus Christ, receives the Holy Spirit. The Holy Spirit works in the life of each believer, building him up in the faith so that he may become conformed to Jesus Christ. The Holy Spirit also integrates each believer into God's plan for the church in the world. The Holy Spirit fills men for power in witnessing. In Acts 4:8 Peter, as he was filled with the Holy Spirit, answered the religious leaders boldly giving them the gospel. In Acts 7:55 the Holy Spirit gave Stephen the power and the ability to be God's first gracious martyr. The journals of Paul the Apostle on his missionary journeys are filled with testimonies of the leading and the empowering of the Holy Spirit.

The Holy Spirit is the giver of gifts to the members of the church for outreach. It is the Holy Spirit who equips the members of the church to carry out its mission in the world. In Acts 8 Philip, guided by the Holy Spirit from the mass ministry in Samaria, successfully brought the gospel to a single individual in Gaza. In Acts 10 Peter became God's instrument under the guidance of the Holy Spirit to open the door of faith to the Gentiles, with the significant conversion of Cornelius.

4. Relating to the World. Jesus is speaking of the Holy Spirit in John 16:8-10 when He says, "And when he is come, he will reprove [convince] the world of sin, and of righteousness, and of judgment: of sin, because they believe not on me; of righteousness, because I go to my Father, and ye see me no more." No human witness has power in and of himself to convict the heart of an unbeliever. It is only the Holy Spirit who can communicate the gospel in convicting power to an unbelieving heart. Convincing men of Jesus Christ as personal Saviour and drawing them to that Saviour is also completely the work of the Holy Spirit.

We have pointed out that Christ is the founder of world missions, and that the Holy Spirit is the power of world missions. Now consider a third point:

The Church the Agent. The word "church" simply means a called-out assembly. So the church is a body of believing people who have been called out of the world, but sent back into the world to do a work for God. We read in II Corinthians 5:19, "God was in Christ, reconciling the world unto himself . . . and hath committed unto us the word of reconciliation." We also read in I Peter 2:9, "But ye are a chosen generation [race], a royal priesthood, a holy nation, a peculiar [God's own] people; that ye should shew forth the praises of him who hath called you out of darkness into his marvellous light."

So the theology of missions must be the theology of the church. For there is only one New Testament church and that is a church sent out by God into the world with a job to do.

1. Characteristics of the Early Church. From the record in Acts and the Epistles, we discern several character-istics of the early church in missions. They were *obedient* to God and to the command of Christ. They were *sensitive* to the Holy Spirit and to His leading. The early church was saturated in *prayer*. They were a prayerful people. The early church was *united*. This mark of loving unity was a great and forceful testimony in the unbelieving community.

2. Strategy of the Early Church. Notice the following elements of strategy and consider them as points of a model for us in missions today.

- There was the witness of all believers. Acts 8:1 and 4 indicate total mobilization.

- There was a recognition of the gifts of the Spirit and a willing acceptance of the responsibilities that the bestowal of those gifts implies.

- There was the constant preaching of the Word, when-ever an audience could be found.

- There was service of a practical nature to those in need (Acts 6:1-7)

- There was use of strategic centers such as Athens, Corinth, Ephesus and even Rome.

- There was the training of disciples (II Timothy 2:2).

- There was follow-up of new believers by visit, through prayer, through sending of representatives, and through follow-up letters.

The New Testament agency for fulfilling the Great Commission of Jesus Christ is *the church.* Because the church is composed in each and every generation of human beings, it has never been absolutely perfect. Mistakes and failures have occurred. But this is no reason to abandon the centrality of the position of the church in the plan and economy of God.

History, the Record of the Church. The history of the church is in reality the history of missions. It is the nature of the gospel to reach out and share God's good news with those who do not know it. This has continually been the heartthrob of the church. Let us briefly consider select illustrations from the historical record of the church.

1. The Moravians. Count Nicolaus Ludwick von-Zinzendorf (1700-1760) was a great leader of the Moravian believers. These Christians were very zealous and effective missionaries. They put a large emphasis on a personal, spiritual relationship to Jesus Christ. The Moravian missionaries fanned out across the world.

2. The Wesleys. These English brothers were contemporaries with Zinzendorf. John and Charles Wesley were touched by God and were used mightily as preachers of the gospel. Not only did revival spread throughout England as a result of their ministry, but there was a significant missionary impulse to their ministry as well. This resulted in the sending out of Christian workers to the New World and the establishment of mission works in the American colonies.

3. The Cambridge Seven. As a result of a visit to Cambridge University in England in 1882 by the American evangelist, Dwight L. Moody, a significant chapter in missions was written. Seven outstanding students at that famous university were not only saved but were moved to apply to the recently established China

Inland Mission. Each of these seven were not only great scholars but well-known sportsmen. C.T. Studd, a student from a very wealthy English family, was the Captain of the undefeated cricket team and a national sports hero. In February of 1885 these seven Cambridge graduates sailed for China.

4. The Haystack Movement. At Williams College in Massachusetts something important happened among students on this side of the Atlantic as far as missions history is concerned. Samuel J. Mills had been converted in "The Great Awakening" of 1798 at the age of 17. This young convert kindled a spiritual spark with fellow students at Williams College. They organized a student prayer group that met regularly outdoors in the campus orchard. One day a sudden thunderstorm struck, and the students took refuge under the shelter of a haystack in the field. There, with the rain pouring down around them, they continued fervent in prayer. It was from this haystack prayer meeting that the foreign missionary movement of the churches of the United States of America had its start. Later, as part of this student missions movement, Adoniram Judson and Samuel Newell with their wives sailed for India. Later Samuel Nott, Gordon Hall and Luther Rice embarked for the Far East. A direct result of this student missionary movement was the founding of Baptist missions in North America.

Summary. When Jesus said that He would build His church and that even the gates of hell should not overcome it, His words were true and have been fulfilled a thousandfold. We have in the pages of the New Testament the essential ingredients for missionary enterprise in each succeeding generation. Jesus Christ is still calling for witnesses to move out from His church to proclaim, to evangelize, and to build His church in all parts of His world. Today witnesses are still wanted. The power supply is still available!

The Need for Missions

Here we come to a tremendously significant issue in missions. What is the reason for all of this theory? What is the target for all of this Christian activity? We have seen that at the center of the Universe is God with His great heart of love which reaches out. What are the objects of this outreaching love? Here we come to the basic consideration for the need of missions.

The Problem of Man's Lostness. Are the non-Christians who die without hearing the gospel of Jesus Christ really lost? Remember, pagans are not exclusively found in the Amazon jungles of South America or in the heartlands of Africa! If people without Jesus Christ in their hearts and lives are to be banished for eternity to hell, how does this square with the Biblical concept of God's love and justice?

The questions are pertinent and continually asked. In many circles, even in the "Christian community," the thought of the heathen being lost and condemned, without an opportunity to hear and respond to the gospel, fires up the indignation of human justice.

A further question that is of utmost significance in this context is, for whom did Jesus Christ die? Was His agony and death necessary? The human race is in the state of lostness. Why else would we have the multiplying of religious systems in all cultures of the world? Why else would we have the sacrificial system present in so many cultures? Why else do we find men of all cultures and of every tribe yearning for completeness, or integration, or relationship to the great spirit of the universe? Why else do we have this seething of nations? Why else do we have the abundance of cruelty and despair in the world? The very presence of sin and of all of these other things is evidence of the state of human lostness.

It has been the business of Christian missions through the ages in all lands and in all generations to help man to escape from this state of lostness and to set the feet of man on the pathway that leads to eternal life.

Consider now another point.

Some Solutions to the Problem. Let us briefly look at some solutions to the dilemma of man before we consider in detail God's solution to the problem.

1. Universalism. This system of belief says that no sinner will escape the saving grace of God, even in spite of himself and his sin. Those who hold to this view say that man is not eternally damned and spiritually lost, but is only blinded. The task of missions therefore is to say to the Hindu or to the Buddhist or to the animist to open his eyes and to recognize the established fact that he is a child of God. This solution would be very comfortable if you turned your mind and heart away from the warnings of the Biblical prophets, of the Lord Jesus Christ Himself, and of the apostles concerning the live option of eternal hell.

2. Salvation only by means of the church. This solution suggests that God's offer of salvation is exclusively through the means of grace deposited in the humanly organized church. This is the Roman Catholic view, and also occurs in certain Protestant denominations. It is based on the notion that salvation is at least in part due to human action. Those individuals who are outside of the church are also outside of heaven and eternal life.

3. Salvation by response to nature's light. This viewpoint observes that because God has given all men the light of nature He will save or condemn individuals, quite apart from the gospel, on the basis of responding to

this natural revelation. There is a subtlety in this viewpoint, as there is in the first two.

4. Salvation through reception of the person of the Lord Jesus Christ. This view states that when an individual human being comprehends the claims of the gospel, and significance of the person and work of God's Son, the Lord Jesus Christ, he receives enabling faith to trust the Lord and to receive God's gift of eternal life. This is God's solution to the problem of man's lostness, as revealed throughout Scripture.

The Exclusiveness of the Gospel. Christian missions declares unequivocally that Jesus Christ is the world's only Saviour. We believe that there is only one way to heaven. This is not to establish a rivalry between religious systems. There is a tremendous difference between religious systems devised and concocted by human minds, and the revealed plan of God from heaven.

A Chinese Christian convert was trying to explain the uniqueness of Christianity to an audience of Confucianists and Buddhists. This Chinese Christian had been both a Confucianist and a Buddhist but had found no satisfactory way until he met Jesus Christ and accepted Him as personal Saviour. To his audience he presented his testimony in the form of a parable. A traveler had fallen off the path of right living into a bog of despair. He tried futilely to save himself. He realized that the suction of the bog would soon destroy him. At this moment Confucius appeared above him on the path of right living. The poor traveler cried, "Save me, Confucius!" The reply came, "That is no place for prayer. You should have kept on the path of right living." And Confucius passed him by.

Then Buddha came along the same path. Again there was the desperate cry for help. Buddha was certainly sympathetic and he bent down and urged the struggling traveler, "Try harder. Raise yourself higher. Raise yourself a little more and maybe I can save you." The man simply could not raise himself a fraction of an inch. His resistance to the suction of the mire and muck of the bog was almost gone.

Then who should come along the path but the Lord Jesus Christ. Immediately He sees the poor man's plight. The struggling fellow can scarcely cry for help now. Jesus sees the pleading look in the poor man's eyes. He descends into the bog Himself, and takes the lost traveler in His arms, and raises him up, and eventually cleans him off and sets him again on the path of right living.

This beautiful parable from the mind of a Chinese Christian says it so well. Jesus Christ is unique. His way is not simply a better way. He is the only actual Way of salvation.

Jesus Christ Himself declared in John 14:6, "No man cometh unto the Father, but by me." The apostles Peter, Paul, and John also confirmed Christ as the only way of salvation (Acts 4:12; I Corinthians 3:11; John 3:36). The term "salvation" pre-supposes a Saviour. A religion without a Saviour is not really a saving religion. The Bible accurately mirrors man's need of a Saviour. It speaks of Christ as the only one personally qualified by His virgin birth and sinless life to be that Saviour for all peoples in all the world. He died because there was no other way (Galatians 3:21). His resurrection from the dead is also unique in all of history, and is a brilliant demonstration of the completeness of God's way of salvation.

Picture the Lord Jesus Christ standing at life's port of embarkation inviting all men to come on board His "Good Ship Grace." He encourages men to sail with Him into unknown ocean of death and judgment to God on the far shore. While He stands and invites all to come on board

He condemns all other "vessels" as mere "paper liners," doomed to destruction and despair. He does this because He knows that only He has sailed into the full fury of God's judgment on sin and has returned to the port of life victorious. Only in Him is there safety. It makes great sense to trust in Jesus the "Captain of our Salvation."

The Way of Salvation Revealed. God has clearly revealed Himself and His way of salvation for humanity. Men are lost or saved, not on the basis of human concepts of "fairness," not even because of any supposed failure on God's part to provide revelation.

Men and women are spiritually lost BECAUSE THEY ARE SINNERS.

1. Natural revelation. God has given *natural* revelation *to* all men. "The heavens declare the glory of God; and the firmament sheweth his handywork" (Psalm 19:1). Romans 1 declares that the wrath of God is revealed from heaven against all forms of sin, because God has shown Himself to the ungodly in His creation of the world, by which they should be able to understand that all things were made by His eternal power. See verses 18 through 20. Then verse 20 ends with the statement, "so that they are without excuse." This speaks to all men, if they will only listen, of God's glory, power, wisdom, and judgment, but not of His saving grace.

2. Special revelation. God has also given *special* revelation *for* all men. This speaks of God's grace, personified in the Lord Jesus Christ, and spelled out in detail in His written revelation, the Scriptures.

Although special revelation is the only effective means by which men are saved, please remember that it is not always effective in producing this salvation. Judas lived with Jesus, yet he was unsaved. Myriads of mankind have been exposed to Scripture without appropriating the way—receiving Jesus Christ and being saved. So revelation itself, whether natural or special, neither saves nor condemns. Responding to the revelation and believing on Christ and receiving Him as Saviour is the essential issue.

How does the human heart respond to the light of God given either in natural revelation or in special revelation? This is the crucial issue. To all men God gives the light of creation, conscience, and providence. To those who respond to this light, He sends the light of the gospel. God deals individually with persons. To the individual who responds positively and gratefully, God unfailingly sends further revelation, if He has to move heaven, or earth, or men to do it!

This is the story of missions! This demonstrates the need for missions.

This principle of God's amazing and sovereign grace at work is demonstrated strategically in Luke's account of three crucial conversions in Acts 8, 9, and 10. They are each highly civilized, lost heathen—the Ethiopian eunuch, Saul of Tarsus, and Cornelius the Roman Centurion.

In each of these three cases salvation results through the sovereign activity of the Holy Spirit preparing the heart of the lost sinner to respond to the light, and also the heart of the witness. These three lost heathen, of greatly divergent cultural and racial backgrounds, (1) responded actively to light given, (2) received the active witness of a prepared messenger, and, (3) fully responded and received the Word of the cross.

The God of missions is the Lord of the harvest. He has an effective plan of bringing to Himself a harvest of lost souls. If lost men are to be saved, and they will be, it must be by the *Word of the cross*. Here is the need for missions.

CHAPTER 6

What Is a "Missionary Call"?

Warren Webster

Few theological topics have been surrounded by more fuzzy thinking and meaningless cliches than that of the "missionary call." The idea has been so overworked it is little wonder that some people are turned off by just the mention of it. Others who have sincerely committed their lives to Christ for service are perplexed as they sit back waiting to be "called."

No one seems to know when or where the term "missionary call" originated. The words are not found in the Bible. Even the concept of a special "missionary call" as a necessary preliminary to serving God in the world is difficult to support from the Scriptures. Through misuse and misunderstanding the idea of such a "call" has been built up into something that simply was not known in the early church.

The Bible reveals a speaking God who summons the earth from the rising of the sun to its setting (see Psalm 50:1). The God who calls men and nations "out of darkness into his marvellous light" (I Peter 2:9) calls them to Himself—for salvation (Acts 2:38,39) and fellowship (I Corinthians 1:9), as well as for discipleship (Mark 1:17) and service (Ephesians 2:10). But the popular use of the word "call" as a prerequisite for Christian service is hard to substantiate from either the direct statements of

Scripture or the biographies of God's servants.

Myths About the "Missionary Call"

For those who seek to know God and to do His will it may prove helpful to dispel some of the myths and misunderstandings about a special "call" to missions.

The myth of Paul's "Macedonian call." There is a common notion that Paul's vision on the way to Macedonia, found in Acts 16:6-10, was part of his "missionary call." It should be noted that the Macedonian vision was not at all part of Paul's introduction to missionary service. Some twelve to fourteen years after his conversion, the Apostle Paul was sent out from the church at Antioch on his first missionary journey (Acts 13). By the time we come to the events of Acts 16 Paul had already completed his first term of service and was halfway through his second missionary journey when he had a vision in the night of a man in Macedonia saying, "Come over . . . and help us."

This came at a time when Paul was already on the move in response to the general obligation to take the gospel where it was not known. He had gone to the limits of his ability to obey the Great Commission of Matthew 28:19,20. Finding that God's time had not yet arrived for the provinces of Asia and Bithynia, he stopped at Troas to wait for God to reveal the next step. There he had his "Macedonian vision." It was an unusual and rather spectacular instance of God directing the next step in Paul's missionary ministries. But it was not a "missionary call" for it took place as part of a missionary career that had begun long before. Moreover, the geographical direction to go to Macedonia was just temporary as Paul did not stay there very long.

The myth of "a mystical experience." An idea persists

that Christ's followers need some mystical experience or extraordinary guidance in order to enter missionary service. But we look in vain for any common factor in the influences which launched New Testament witnesses on their mission.

Following the stoning of Stephen, God used *persecution* to scatter scores of nameless disciples as witnesses throughout Judea and Samaria (Acts 8:1). Some of them went as far as Phoenicia, Cyprus and Antioch (Acts 11:19). Those who had been scattered preached the Word wherever they went (Acts 8:4). There is no indication that those early witnesses had any special "call" or mystical guidance telling them where to go with the gospel. They probably went first to sympathetic friends and relatives in the towns and cities from which they had originally come. God simply used persecution to disperse them on a mission to the hills of Judea and Samaria and regions beyond, wherever they went they were missionaries of the gospel.

Philip was one of the early disciples dispersed to Samaria where he preached good news about Christ and the kingdom of God (Acts 8:5,12). Later when the Lord wanted Philip to witness cross-culturally to an Ethiopian official he used an *angel* to direct Philip to the right place (Acts 8:26-28).

Shortly after the conversion of Paul, God sent a *man,* Ananias, to inform Saul that he was chosen to be a witness before Gentiles and kings and his fellow Jews (Acts 9:15).

Some years later when Paul had proven himself ready for a ministry to Gentiles, the Holy Spirit directed the *church leaders* in Antioch to send Paul and Barnabas on their first missionary journey.

The motivating factor in Paul's second missionary journey seemed to be a natural sense of responsibility to revisit the churches he and Barnabas had established: "Let us go again and visit our brethren in every city where we have preached the word of the Lord, and see how they do" (Acts 15:36).

When Paul and Barnabas decided to lead separate mission bands to different places "Paul chose Silas" as a companion (Acts 15:40). Silas apparently went because *another missionary chose* him and then the local believers commended him to the service of the Lord.

In all of these instances we find a common commitment to the Lordship of Christ and the extension of his kingdom. But apart from that each passage reveals a different influence leading to missionary involvement. The conclusion is that the Lord has no set pattern for leading His people into missionary service. Apart from a total commitment to Christ and to world evangelization we should not be surprised if every missionary has a unique experience of God's direction for service.

The myth of "every Christian a missionary." One popular misconception about missionary ministries is expressed by the slogan: "Every heart with Christ, a missionary; every heart without Christ, a mission field."

Of course, what is meant is that every real Christian is—or ought to be—a witness for the Lord. With that we would heartily agree. But that is very different from saying, "Every Christian is a missionary." A little reflection should make the difference clear.

In the first place, when God had a special job to be done in the Mediterranean world he did not send the whole church at Antioch. He simply chose two key leaders from that assembly, Paul and Barnabas. There is no indication that God wanted, or intended, that more than those two should go. The Lord does not normally expect a mass migration of believers from one city or country to another. He is not looking for a vast spiritual "fruit basket upset" in which all American Christians should go to Asia, with all Japanese believers migrating to the Philippines and all Filipino Christians coming to the United States.

Missionaries have always been in the minority, like Paul and Barnabas who were the only two initially chosen from the church at Antioch. Even among our Lord's many disciples only twelve of the hundred and twenty or so in Jerusalem were "sent ones," or apostles. The Greek word *apostolos* means "one sent forth" on a special task. God's special "sent ones" in every age have been a small fraction of his total people. But at their best they have been an "overwhelming minority"—the kind of dynamic disciples God uses to "turn the world upside down" (Acts 17:6)! All believers are to be witnesses where they are. Only a minority will be sent to work and witness among culturally different people.

It is furthermore quite apparent from the Bible's teaching about "spiritual gifts" that every Christian is not a missionary. Just as not every part of the body is an eye, so not every member of the Body of Christ is an evangelist. First Corinthians 12 indicates that not all of the early Christians were apostles or prophets. No one today believes that every Christian is a pastor, or that all believers have the gift of teaching. Likewise, all Christians do not have the ability and adaptability to learn and effectively use another language or to live and witness in another culture.

The word missionary is derived from the Latin noun *missio* ("a sending out") from which we get the English word "mission." A missionary then is "one sent out on a mission"—especially a mission to preach, teach and spread some cause. It is understandable that no occurrences or derivatives of this basically Latin word are found in the New Testament which was inspired and recorded in Greek. Interestingly enough, however, the

Latin-derived word "missionary" and the Greek-derived
word "apostle" mean almost exactly the same, that is, "one
sent out with a specific task." Because of historical and
cultural developments since the first century, modern
missionaries cannot be directly equated with Biblical
apostles and evangelists. But a contemporary church-
planting missionary generally combines in his life and
ministry characteristics of both New Testament apostles
and evangelists as he crosses cultural and/or geographical boundaries to proclaim Christ, enlisting and
training disciples as responsible members of reproducing
churches.

Understanding then that a missionary is "one sent out
with a specific task" we can distinguish missionaries
from others carrying out important functions within the
Body of Christ.

A missionary has a specific task. He ministers in a
structured, rather than a casual, witnessing situation. All
Christians should seek to be witnesses to those whom they
casually meet in the course of their everyday lives.
Missionaries do this too, but they are sent out on a
"specific task" with goals for evangelizing a whole city or
area where they expect God to multiply believers and
churches.

A missionary is sent, not called, to his work. Churches
"call" pastors and evangelists to come and minister in
their midst. In so doing they accept the responsibility for
supporting those servants of Christ whom they invite to
teach and lead the flock. Missionaries, who are sent to
their work, minister to peoples who do not support them
and may not even want the message of repentance and
reconciliation which they go to proclaim.

A missionary generally crosses significant boundaries
of culture or language, or both, in fulfilling his task.
Missionaries are sent out—away from home, family,

nation, people and the customs and culture they best understand. Like Abraham, they go to a place of God's direction, generally going without previous experience in the area where they are to serve. They go to people in great need and they do it for Christ's sake and the gospel.

The myth of a "different kind of call." Another myth that needs dispelling is the idea that a Christian needs some special call for missions that he doesn't need for, say, teaching school in America.

Actually, God's leading into missionary service is not essentially different from His direction to anything else. Every Christian should be concerned to ascertain the will of God and follow it. In this process it is more important to begin with vocation than location.

Far too great a distinction has generally been made between so-called secular and sacred ("full-time Christian service" vocations). Every legitimate occupation should have a Christian dimension. Some vocations may be more significant than others for wielding key Christian influence, but young people should be sensitive to the Biblical dimensions in all vocations.

In deciding on a career, a Christian should carefully and prayerfully evaluate his talents, tastes, aptitudes and abilities—both natural and spiritual. This should be done in the light of community and world needs and the resources available to meet those needs. Christians should consider the Lord's priorities, not simply their own. In view of God's plan and Christ's command that the whole world should hear the gospel, some type of personal involvement in world evangelization ought to be seriously considered by every believer.

Don't be surprised if God leads you to give up what you think is a "normal" means of livelihood in order to follow His direction for your life. Jesus left the carpenter's shop to go on His mission. His earliest disciples left their nets to follow Him. And Paul left regular tent-making to become a missionary.

Choose your life's involvement wisely, prayerfully, and with the evangelization of the world in view. The most important thing is knowing God's will for you—and doing it! David Bentley-Taylor, a missionary to Indonesia, expressed it this way: "Whether you are going to spend your life in your own country or abroad you need that sense of the knowledge of God's will. There is no scriptural ground for saying you need a specific type of call to overseas service which you don't need for service at home. The distinction between a call to South America and a call to Southern California is geographical, not spiritual."

The myth of "once a missionary, always a missionary." There is a common conception that missionary service is for life. Is that true? While every Christian ought to be a lifelong witness for Jesus Christ it does not necessarily follow that a person's entire lifetime will be spent living and witnessing in another culture. Even the Apostle Paul returned on "furloughs" to Antioch and Jerusalem to report what God was doing in other places.

The concept "once a missionary always a missionary" may go back to the example of men like William Carey who served Christ in India for 40 years and died there without ever returning to his home and relatives in England. Similarly, Adoniram Judson's first term of service in India and Burma lasted 33 years! But these were exceptions, perhaps due as much to the difficulties and delays in transcontinental travel during that era as to the deep commitment of the men themselves. Vast distances that took Carey and Judson weeks and months to travel are now covered in just hours by missionaries traveling by plane, making the older patterns unnecessary and irrelevant.

But the question remains, apart from improved global transportation and shortened terms of service must missionary service be exclusively a lifetime commitment?

The Apostle Paul died in missionary service, as did Carey, Judson and many others from that day to this. Little is known, however, about the subsequent careers of Paul's missionary companions. Did Luke, the physician, continue his missionary journeys after Paul's death, or did he retire to write and practice medicine? We don't know. How long did Barnabas continue in missionary service after leaving to go on a second missionary journey of his own? The Bible gives us no clue as to the duration of his ministry. We do know that John Mark quit in the middle of his first term of service, but later returned to accompany his cousin Barnabas on a second tour (Acts 15:37-39). But the Scriptures are silent as to whether these men and others of Paul's evangelistic companions, such as Timothy and Titus, continued in missionary service for a lifetime or turned to other ministries. The Apostle John who was active in the mission to Judea and Samaria was later exiled to Patmos and finally, according to tradition, retired to Ephesus where he died.

While the Biblical data is somewhat inconclusive it seems remarkably parallel to what has been experienced in the history of missions. Some of the early New Testament missionaries died in the course of duty, others after retirement from active ministry. Some went on just one or two missionary journeys and then turned to other Christian ministries and vocations. It is the same today.

Where modern missionaries spend much time and effort to learn difficult languages and adapt to diverse cultures they are seldom quickly led to leave the work they have begun. There may be considerable mobility, however, for missionaries within a common linguistic area as in the

Spanish speaking, French speaking, or Arabic speaking regions.

While Christians at home have become accustomed to pastors resigning to take another church, or Christian teachers moving to teach in another school or seminary, many have been unwilling to apply the same principles to missionaries who are led to take a stateside pastorate, teach on a school faculty, serve on the headquarter's staff of a mission, or stay home to marry or take care of family responsibilities.

Biblically speaking the only lifetime commitment one makes is not to a ministry or to a place, but to the will of God. Knowing and doing the will of God must be the Christian's life time commitment. The center of God's will—wherever it may lead—is the pathway of greatest blessing and the safest place for any disciple to walk. The duration or permanency of any particular ministry can be left to the Lord.

Peter Cameron Scott, the founder of the Africa Inland Mission, spent just a little over a year in the field of Kenya. He didn't plan it that way. God called him home just as he was beginning his missionary career. Only a year in Kenya—but for him it was a lifetime of service! This suggests that God is more interested in the quality of a life's commitment than simply in commitment for a lifetime.

The "myth of mediocrity." Some people have an idea that if you can't do anything else you can always be a missionary. The truth is almost exactly the opposite. If you don't have what it takes to succeed in ministry or service at home it is very unlikely that God wants you abroad.

A Christian student from Africa was telling a midwestern church about the spread of Christianity in his country. Afterwards a well-meaning listener came up to him to say, "I've been thinking I might like to serve the Lord in Africa myself."

"What," inquired the speaker, "are you doing now?"

"Not much of anything," came the reply.

"Then, please," said the speaker, "don't go to Africa to do it!"

The confrontation with pagan ideologies, resurgent ethnic religions and anti-Christian opposition in many countries overseas requires the strongest and best of God's people. The pressures are enough to challenge the keenest mind and the deepest spiritual commitment. Cross-cultural evangelism is not holier, but it is generally harder. It requires all the skills and abilities needed to minister among your own people plus facility in cross-cultural adaption and communication. Humanly speaking, one of the most challenging things you can ever do is leave the land and culture of your birth, where you know the language and understand people, in order to carry the gospel to a place where you may have to begin all over again like a child to learn a new language and customs. Not everyone can do it.

For every Christian who can make the adjustments necessary to function effectively in another culture there are probably nine or ten who couldn't but who can have a significant ministry at home. It is not wrong to aim high. If you think you have what it takes, then consider cross-cultural missions. Pray for the privilege of serving the Lord where the needs and challenges are greatest and where workers and resources for evangelizing and discipling are most limited. If God doesn't ultimately open doors for you in that direction you can be sure He will find places for you to minister at home. But the insights gained in preparing for cross-cultural evangelism will make you a better "world Christian" wherever you service.

Truths About Missionary Service

Dick Hillis, a veteran missionary to Asia, confesses that he was never "called" to China, although he served there as a missionary for eighteen years. Like the Apostle Paul, the Lord called him primarily to a work rather than a place. He says God gave him the gifts, or calling, of teaching. For some years he used that ability in China for the edification of the Body of Christ there. When China closed he continued to use his gift of teaching in other parts of Asia and the Americas. The following truths about missionary service make it clear that when it comes to the game of life, the stadium you play in is not nearly as important as being on a winning team, with the right Captain, and playing for all you are worth.

In the Christian life our primary calling is to a Person. The Lord calls us, like the earliest disciples, first to be with Him and then to be sent out to preach (Mark 3:14). Our commitment to Christ is permanent and lasts a lifetime.

The basis for all Christian service is a threefold commitment to the Lordship of Christ. First in importance is total commitment to follow Christ as Head of the church (Ephesians 1:22). Next in order is commitment to the church as the Body of Christ, and to one another within the fellowship of believers (Ephesians 4:15,16). The Christian's third commitment is to the service of Christ in the world (Ephesians 2:10).

Involvement in world evangelization begins with Biblical convictions. The Bible is a missionary book from beginning to end. God is concerned for all peoples everywhere because He created them, and He so loved them that He gave His only begotten Son so they might not perish because of their sin, but have everlasting life by believing on the Son (John 3:16). But they need someone to tell them the Good News—"how shall they hear without a preacher?" (Romans 10:14). Even now God is calling out "a people for his name" (Acts 15:14) which ultimately will include some from tribe and tongue and people and nation (Revelation 5:9).

God guides people primarily in terms of their work of ministry. The place is secondary. When the Holy Spirit said, in Acts 13:2, that the church was to set apart Barnabas and Saul unto Him "for the work whereunto I have called them," they were not being directed to a geographical location in Europe or Asia but to the work of preaching and teaching.

God guides through natural abilities and spiritual gifts. God gifts people for ministry and then guides them in using those gifts to the glory of Christ. We should understand that one set of gifts and abilities may provide the basis for a number of different ministries or callings at different times. In developing our gifts and abilities we should remember that the New Testament has even more to say about Christian character than about spiritual gifts. God is concerned with what we are—and are becoming—as well as with what we can do. The "fruit of the Spirit" (Galatians 5:22,23) is as important as the gifts of the Spirit. When life and characters are right for ministry God can, and often does, supply what is needed to meet the challenge of waiting opportunities.

Be aware, however, that God does not always guide in terms of natural abilities. Talent is not the ultimate indication of what the Lord wants you to do. If you are athletic, or scholarly, or musical you should develop and use those talents and abilities but you should not assume that your calling and vocation will necessarily be along those lines. While relationships of natural ability to one's ministry is often close or complementary, it should not be taken for granted. God may gift and guide you into spiritual ministries which are very different.

The choice of your career is one of the three most important decisions you will make in life. It is next in importance only to your acceptance of Christ, and equal in significance with your choice of a life partner. In marrying, seek a Christian partner who will be a strength and help wherever the Lord leads. Many young people impair any possibility of an effective Christian ministry by marrying unwisely or contrary to God's standards and revealed will. They should make this important decision wisely, prayerfully, and with the evangelization of the world in mind.

The Spirit of God does give a special direction or guidance for missionary service. It is not for everyone. Just as people come to Christ in many different ways, so God uses many means of guiding His children into places of service. As the experienced missionary David Bently-Taylor put it: "The way in which God's call is communicated varies with every individual . . . And yet through all the superficial dissimilarity of circumstances there is a common denominator and that is the continual sense that a certain course is God's will for me and that I must do that and not anything else."

CHAPTER 7

The Importance
of NOW

Norman Wetther

"What you are going to be you are now becoming."
What we think and do today has more significance on our future life and character than often we realize. The foundation for that great missionary beginning some years from now—in Central America, Indonesia or urban Chicago—is being built from the materials you put into it a day at a time now.

Let's check into the importance of *now* in our missionary thinking. We were thrilled when three men were thrust into space from planet earth in a powerful and sophisticated spacecraft. We were even more excited when their moon vehicle touched down on that lonely, barren planet and our fellow-earthmen got out and walked around. That lovely bright object in the sky that we had enjoyed so much with that special friend on a warm, clear night now had people walking on it!

Almost unbelievable!

But that exciting landing would never have taken place in that particular moment in time without years of intelligent planning, diligent workmanship and flawless materials. A miscalculation in the basic plan, the negligence of a key employee or a weakness in a critical metal and the whole operation could have failed.

It is exciting to know that we have put a man on the

moon, but it is vastly more exciting to communicate the gospel of Jesus Christ to people who have hell or heaven as their ultimate option. The commitment, the planning, the life-style of our lives today determine what success we will have for Christ in the future. Decisions that we (and others) consider to be greatly significant and slightly earth-shaking are not made in a vacuum. Right decisions made in a time of crisis do not just happen. They are the results of our values (the things that matter most to us), habit-patterns and thinking that we have developed over a period of years.

Remember Daniel in the Bible? As a young man he had a lot going for him. He was intelligent, good-looking, sharp in every way. He and some of his Israeli friends were to receive three years of education in a foreign country. They would live in the capital city and eat the food of the nation's leaders. Yet, because he was involved with a godless nation, Daniel made up his mind that he would not defile himself with the king's choice food or with the wine the king drank (Daniel 1:8). Because Daniel made this kind of a decision as a young man, God used him in a remarkable way as an adult (when he got to his mission field) in a critical period of his nation's history.

A high school sophomore who lived across the street from our family began to attend a Bible study that we were having for Navy and Air Force men on the Island of Guam. He listened attentively, he took notes, on Saturdays he helped to mow the lawn at our Servicemen's Center, he attended each church service because he wanted to. One Sunday evening he publicly acknowledged to the congregation that he was committing his life for the ministry of Jesus Christ. He went on to college and seminary. Today he has a graduate degree and is being used of God in an overseas teaching ministry. Because he was faithful in little things during his high school years,

God allowed him to move on to greater things.

What are the materials that we need to be building into our lives now, the stuff of which a meaningful life and ministry results down the line? The most important of these have to do with the inner life in the area of convictions and attitudes.

Commitment to Christ NOW

Basic to all else is your acceptance of Jesus Christ as Saviour and Lord. This comes only from knowing who He is and believing that everything revealed about Him in the Bible is absolutely true. One must be convinced that He is the only answer to the sin problem in the world and the only means whereby people can be reconciled to God. We never become excited about a cause unless we really believe it is right.

Because He is a gracious God, our heavenly Father has given to us His Spirit to convince us that these things are true. "The Spirit itself beareth witness with our spirit, that we are the children of God" (Romans 8:16). Jesus had promised, "When he, the Spirit of truth is come, he will guide you into all truth . . ." (John 16:13). As we are genuinely open to believe His truth, we can be sure that God Himself will give to us the deep conviction that Jesus Christ is Lord. He is worth dying for, and undoubtedly more relevant to the greater majority of us, He is worth living for.

This means no hang-up on authority concerning who is in charge of our lives. Jesus Christ must be Number One. In every period of man's long history there has been an ego response to the spirit of the songs, "I've Got To Be Me," and "I Did It My Way." The young committed Christian on the other hand responds, "I want to do it His way."

Because Jesus is Lord of the universe He is worth our

best.. Recently I heard a keen Christian young man speak about his future. He had asked himself the question, "How can I best invest my life?" His conclusion was to identify completely with Jesus Christ, to be at His disposal in a life commitment. During infantry training in the Army I vividly recall hearing our sergeant bring us the encouraging news that 2 per cent of our company would be killed in training, that we were expendable for our country. I could appreciate that during a war, but to be expendable for Jesus Christ is far greater. Mediocrity through limited commitment or half-hearted obedience has no place in the life of the servant of Jesus Christ. The battle is too serious, the objective too critical, the outcome too final.

An outstanding example of commitment to Christ that resulted in a Christian witness that shook the nation of China was the testimony of Hudson Taylor at the age of seventeen: "For what service I was accepted I knew not, but a deep consciousness that I was not my own took possession of me which has never since been effaced" (*Hudson Taylor's Spiritual Secret*, by Dr. and Mrs. Howard Taylor).

Attitudes NOW

Inner beliefs determine outward behavior. Right attitudes result in right acts. The Christian who wants his life to count for God must have wholesome attitudes in at least three basic areas of relationships—attitude toward God, toward himself and toward others.

One must believe that God is good, that He is wise and that He does not make any mistakes. Being good, He will not ask His child to do anything which is wrong or too difficult. Paul Little put it well in his message to students at URBANA 1973, "God's Will for Me and World Evangelism": "When we come to God and say 'I love you, and I am prepared to do your will whatever you want me to do,' we can be sure that God is not going to make us miserable. Rather He rejoices and fits our lives into His pattern for us, into that place where He, in His omniscience and love, knows we will fit hand in glove. The one who is our Creator, who made us, who knows us better than we will ever know ourselves, is the one we are talking to. He knows the end from the beginning."

Having settled the matter of our attitude toward God in a simple, yet deep, truth relationship, we need also to have a positive opinion of ourselves. Too often we push the humility stance to an extreme that our Lord never intended. An inadequate understanding of humility can result in a very low estimate of ourselves, our capabilities and our worth. On the other hand a wholesome self-esteem is not to be equated with self-centeredness. God considered that we were worth the death of His Son. If we have received His Son in sincere faith, then we have been accepted by the Creator of the universe. The Apostle Paul put it beautifully: "He that spared not his own Son, but delivered him up for us all, how shall he not with him also freely give us all things?" (Romans 8:32). We are meant to become all that we were made to be through His grace in our lives.

And equally important we must have the right attitude toward others. All people are precious in the sight of the Lord; Christ died for all. It is foolish to plan on a missionary career in Africa if we have an unchristian attitude toward Blacks or Mexicans or Italians or anyone else in our own neighborhood or our own campus. As we begin to expose ourselves to people of other cultures on a personal level now, we become aware, sometimes slowly, at other times in a devastating and humiliating moment, that we have prejudices of which we were not even aware.

Are you concerned about people living in poverty in the

cities of our own nation? Do you hurt for people of another color or ethnic background who are exploited by selfish uncaring apartment owners? The Apostle Paul reminds us that a Christian is to "weep with those who weep." It is not enough to have a vision for people overseas to whom I will go when I become a missionary some day. I must face the reality of human beings without Christ and without hope where I am in this immediate present.

There are exciting opportunities to learn and serve people of other cultures not very far away. Do you have a genuine love for people regardless of their social or economic status or color of skin? Have you considered spending your vacation with a respected missionary in a cross-cultural situation in one of our large cities or on an Indian reservation or in Mexico? Have you initiated a friendship with a foreign exchange student on your campus? This kind of learning and serving involvement among people of other cultures for Jesus' sake today will prepare you well for your mission field of tomorrow.

Personal Relationship with God NOW

The quality of our service *for* Christ is determined in a large measure upon our relationship *with* Christ. A vital, born-again, living relationship with Him implies movement. It is impossible to stand still spiritually. Either we are growing or deteriorating. It is vital to appropriate now the ingredients for growth.

Let the Word of God be real every day. Sunday study alone is not sufficient for significant growth. I once asked a missionary friend how he kept his own relationship with God fresh when he was constantly giving out to others. His answer was clear and brief: "I spend time in the Word and in prayer every day whether I get a charge out of it or not."

Every day? A seminary professor shocked us one day in class when he said, "I don't have time to read the Bible every day." After a pause he continued, "I have to make time." We must believe that it is absolutely necessary. Jesus promised, "Blessed are they which do hunger and thirst after righteousness: for they shall be filled" (Matthew 5:6). Develop a plan of reading and studying the Word and stick to it daily.

Pray daily. Jesus said that the foremost commandment of all is to "love the Lord thy God with all thy heart, and with all thy soul, and with all thy mind, and with all thy strength" (Mark 12:30). This quality of love *from* us, as a result of the Calvary love of Christ for us, will cause us to *want* to have fellowship with Him. Planned times for prayer daily are necessary, but "without ceasing" prayer (I Thessalonians 5:17) is also vital. An English minister said it well: "The Spirit of prayer is even better than the habit of prayer."

Desire to know the will of God for your life now as well as for your future. He has a plan for your life, not only for your vocation later, but for today and tomorrow as well. Someone has said that a qualification for knowing God's will for the future is doing His will as we know it now: wanting to live as Jesus lived, to react to problems as He reacted, to relate to people as He related, and to know and do the Father's will as He did.

Keep on believing. The Apostle Paul counseled the Colossian Christians, "As ye have therefore received Christ Jesus the Lord, so walk ye in him" (Colossians 2:6). We realize that the only way to receive Him as Lord and Saviour is by faith. Paul says that is the way to walk as well. No matter how tough things get or how much you tend to be discouraged, keep trusting your Heavenly

Father who loves you very much and will not permit you to be tested beyond the endurance that He will provide. Job's faith is almost unbelievable when he cries out, "Though he slay me, yet will I trust in him" (Job 13:15). That's keeping on believing.

Be Involved in Church NOW

The church is precious in God's sight. Jesus stated that He would build His church and that the gates of Hades would not overpower it. Paul spoke of "the church of God, which he hath purchased with his own blood" (Acts 20:28). The church should be valued by every Christian.

But young people often ask, and some older ones too, "Which church?" It should be a local body of Christian believers who accept the Bible as God's Word as completely trustworthy for faith and life, and who acknowledge Jesus Christ as Lord and Saviour, the Head of the Church. It should be a church where a concern for evangelism and missions is evident in the emphasis of pastor and people.

Christian missions does not stop with evangelism, but has as its ultimate goal committed believers gathered together to form reproducing churches. The assembled local church is found in the same Bible as the Great Commission.

What does this mean to you now as a Christian? The Bible teaches that when we receive Christ, we are to be baptized. The Christian wants others to know that he has identified himself with Jesus, that he has become one of His followers. This public witness to our faith was commanded by Jesus Himself within His well-known missionary mandate to "Make disciples of all nations." This is one of our first evidences to the world that Jesus has become Lord of our lives.

Identification with the local church follows identification with Christ. There is no perfect church on earth because the church is people, and even born-again people are not yet perfect. However, believers need the supportive relationship of each other as they move on to maturity. They pray for one another, encourage one another, love one another and build up one another. They exercise the gifts that Christ has given, strengthening the church and making known God's love to lost people.

With other believers in the church, Christians continually remember the expensive price of their salvation through partaking of the Lord's Supper. In the Communion Service we are reminded that although redemption is free to the acceptor, it was costly to the Saviour. "This is my body," Jesus said, "which is given for you: this do in remembrance of me. . . . This cup is the new testament [covenant] in my blood, which is shed for you" (Luke 22:19,20). Christians remember together their crucified, risen Lord in the church and give thanks.

And it is in and through the church that we serve the Lord in using our spiritual gifts on behalf of others. Some teach, some usher, some sing, some visit the aged and lonely people, others help in numerous other ministries. In serving others God gives us a deep sense of satisfaction— "whosoever shall lose his life for my sake and the gospel's, the same shall save it" (Mark 8:35)—and at the same time we are learning to be His servants. If you are committed to a Biblical concept of the church now, it is likely that the local church will receive its proper emphasis in your ministry if you go to a mission field later.

Share Your Faith NOW

One of the most important questions asked of a missionary candidate when he appears before an interviewing committee is: "What success have you had in leading others to Christ?" The oft-repeated statement,

"Crossing the ocean does not make a missionary," is true. A missionary candidate may have done many good things in the church through college and seminary years, but if there has been little or no concern for personal sharing of this faith with others, it is very unlikely that this will change later, if or when he is appointed and sent to people of another culture.

Every Christian should master God's plan of redemption, know where to turn in the Bible for key salvation scriptures, and know how to share this Good News in a meaningful way with others. The names of non-Christian friends and relatives should be upon our hearts and come before the Lord in compassionate intercession continually. We must identify with Christ's compassion which caused Him "to seek and to save that which was lost."

A young Navy man of my acquaintance related how he was challenged by the words of Jesus recorded in John 14:15: "If ye love me, keep my commandments." He did love his new Master and wanted to evidence His love through an obedient Christian life. He began to search in the Bible for the commandments of Jesus. One in particular gripped Him: "Go ye therefore, and teach [make disciples of] all nations . . ." (Matthew 28:19a). He struggled in his mind as to how he could keep this commandment. It would be impossible for him to go to every nation. As he thought and prayed about it, he began to find some answers.

He would begin by sharing his faith with his circle of friends near him. He would write his testimony in letters to family and Navy buddies in other areas. He would tithe his income to assist in sending God's servants to other nations. He would get acquainted with a few missionaries and their needs and pray for them daily. He began to develop a small but select library of booklets and salvation tracts that he would share wisely with others. This is a tremendous example of taking evangelism seriously *now*, rather than waiting for a formal appointment and the crossing of an ocean as a "missionary."

Growing in Knowledge NOW

There is no place for mediocrity in the Christian life and on the mission field. It was written of Jesus concerning His young life, "The child grew, and waxed strong in spirit, filled with wisdom: and the grace of God was upon him" (Luke 2:40). Our bodies and minds, with their astounding potential, are gifts from God to be developed by us with deliberate care.

A Christian who develops good reading habits while still in school and after will reap continuing benefits for his entire life, not only in the area of personal enjoyment, but also toward Christian maturity and spiritual effectiveness. Biographies have done more to shape my missionary thinking and attitudes than any reading other than the Bible. There are hundreds of excellent books written about the lives of missionaries and other men and women of God. Helpful books and periodicals on the subject of missions and cross-cultural studies are also readily available. A wise pastor, a respected Christian friend, or a missionary would be happy to recommend specific titles.

Careful listening to a pastor's sermon, Sunday School lesson, or a missionary speaker will also contribute to intellectual growth. Related to good listening is the taking of careful notes and re-study of the material. A young woman who had completed medical school and hospital internship applied to a mission board for appointment as a medical missionary. Normally a mission board would require Bible school or seminary training in addition to her medical training. But because it had been her habit to take notes on sermons and Bible studies since she was in high school, she had acquired such a knowledge of the Word that the interviewing board waived the Bible study requirement. She is an example of outstanding individual effort, not mediocrity.

This is not to recommend bypassing formal Bible training in preparation for missionary service. For an effective ministry among tomorrow's peoples where Third World cultures are placing a great emphasis on literacy and education, a missionary must be well-equipped to share meaningfully the gospel of Jesus Christ.

Outstanding individual effort by today's youth is seen constantly on the athletic field, in music, in Olympic competition. Why not for Jesus? Complete commitment to Christ coupled with wholesome attitudes, a growing relationship with God, a meaningful involvement in a local church, a warm sincere evangelistic outreach and a maturing mind today will produce missionaries who will be used of God to transform lives over all the world tomorrow.

CHAPTER 8

The Missionary and His Mission Board

Richard Lindemann

We have all watched or participated in a football game. Can you imagine the team members gathered in a huddle setting up the next play, then breaking that huddle with all the team except the quarterback returning to the sidelines as spectators? Hardly! The quarterback would be literally squashed.

This illustrates the necessity of teamwork between a missionary and his mission board. The missionary standing alone, like that unfortunate quarterback, very likely would be "squashed"—physically, economically, spiritually and morally. The development of a joyful and effective working relationship is an absolute "must" for the missionary and his mission board. Their goal is to function as members of the same team reaching for a singular goal.

To fully understand this necessary relationship, we will have to consider the meaning of two words: *responsibility* and *accountability*. These words can be understood from the way the New Testament church in the book of Acts developed their missions program and from how church history confirmed God's plan.

The New Testament Pattern

Responsibility. The responsibility for the sending and

93

maintaining of missionaries was given to the local church. As the missionary force grew in numbers and as missionary costs and coordination grew in need, local churches had to combine their efforts. We want to see how these Biblical responsibilities developed in the early church.

There are at least four major responsibilities that the church has toward its missionaries, as illustrated in the Bible.

1. *Preparation of Prayer.* "And when they had fasted and prayed, and laid their hands on them, they sent them away" (Acts 13:3). Significant spiritual events always follow prayer. Also study Acts 2:41-47; 4:31-33; Ephesians 6:18-20. A challenging study would be to look up each place in the book of Acts where prayer is used. See how missions and missionaries become dynamic as a result of prayer.

2. *Picking of Candidates.* The Holy Spirit works in and through the local church leaders. "Now there were in the church that was at Antioch certain prophets and teachers. . . as they ministered to the Lord, and fasted, the Holy Ghost said, Separate me Barnabas and Saul for the work whereunto I have called them" (see Acts 13:1-4). Study these verses and find how the leaders of the church in Antioch and the Spirit of God worked together in selecting Paul and Barnabas.

It is also noteworthy to see that God places this awesome responsibility on the church leaders. The missionary didn't just "volunteer" to go. Think about this approach to becoming a missionary. Thus far, it involves prayer, fasting, and the Holy Spirit working through the church leaders as well as the missionary being willing. Are we really following this pattern today? Also read

Romans 16 and see the list of Missionary Paul's "fellow-workers."

3. *Placing of Missionaries.* The church leaders were of "one mind" in sending the missionaries. "It seemed good unto us, being assembled with one accord, to send chosen men unto you with our beloved Barnabas and Paul. . ." (Acts 15:25-27). Again the church in total agreement sent their missionaries out and gave them instructions of how to minister. Also read Ephesians 6:21,22 and Colossians 1:4-8 for further examples.

4.*Putting Forth Funds.* Consistent giving and diverse application was the pattern as seen in Acts 11:27-30. "Then the disciples, every man according to his ability, determined to send relief unto the brethren which dwelt in Judea. . ." (verse 29). The church saw the need for famine relief. Notice that they distributed the money through their missionaries.

The church accepted its responsibility to financially support its missionaries. "But I rejoiced in the Lord greatly, that now at the last your care of me hath flourished. . .for even in Thessalonica ye sent once and again unto my necessity" (Philippians 4:10,15,16).

The church reached out to the needy. "For it hath pleased them of Macedonia and Achaia to make a certain contribution for the poor saints which are at Jerusalem" (Romans 15:26). Notice that the needy were in Jerusalem where the church originally started. Daughter churches were now reaching out to help the mother church that was in need.

Accountability. As the churches continued to fulfill their responsibility to their missionaries, the missionaries too felt their need to be accountable to their supporting churches and to promote further mission enterprise.

1. *Reports*. The missionaries reported what the Lord had done. "Then all the multitude kept silence, and gave audience to Barnabas and Paul, declaring what miracles and wonders God had wrought among the Gentiles by them. . ." (Acts 15:12-23).

2. *Exhortation*. Missionary Paul exhorted his young disciple to further good works. "Thou therefore, my son, be strong in the grace that is in Christ Jesus. And the things that thou hast heard of me among many witnesses, the same commit thou to faithful men, who shall be able to teach others also. Thou therefore endure hardness, as a good soldier of Jesus Christ" (II Timothy 2:1-3). See also II Timothy 4:1-5.

3. *Involvement*. Missionary Paul continued to involve himself with his churches in ministry. "And I myself also am persuaded of you, my brethren, that ye also are full of goodness, filled with all knowledge, able also to admonish one another. Nevertheless, brethren, I have written the more boldly unto you. . ." (Romans 15:14-20).

Development Through Church History

The period following that of the apostles became increasingly lacking in missionary endeavors. We hear of no outstanding missionary leaders, but individual believers continued to carry the gospel message wherever they went. Eventually, but only within recent history beginning with the nineteenth century, the need for worldwide evangelization was reawakened in the churches. Through time and experience, it became necessary to organize mission societies or boards to carry on the work of missions. These societies were formed in order to help the churches meet the needs of missionaries better, and to help the missionaries do a more effective job.

Relation to the Missionary

Having studied the Biblical relationship of *responsibility* and *accountability* between the local church and the missionary, we are better prepared to answer pertinent questions concerning the missionary and his mission board.

Is the Mission Board really necessary? When the first missionaries were sent out, one local church was responsible. As the missionary force expanded and more mission fields were entered, it no longer was possible for one church to handle the responsibility. Soon it was apparent that the churches needed to join their financial efforts in order to support more missionaries. The next logical and necessary step was the forming of a mission board run by representatives of the local churches.

The mission board handles the finances that churches contribute and assists the churches in determining if certain Christian workers are qualified to serve as missionaries. The mission board also assists the qualified missionary in making contact with new churches.

Perhaps one of the most strategic ministries the mission board performs is to help the missionary coordinate and direct his ministry with other missionaries overseas. This effort saves duplication of much effort and materials, thus saving the churches thousands of dollars each year.

The mission board also produces literature, such as magazines, brochures, study guides and seminar materials to help both the church and the missionary serve and minister to one another. Many mission boards also contribute to the graduate and post-graduate training of their missionaries.

It is important to note that many countries today won't accept a missionary entering their country on a permanent basis unless he is sponsored by a recognized mission society. So, current government regulations become a factor.

With all these things in mind, we can see the necessity and desirability of the mission board or society.

What is a personalized support program and why should it be used? Some mission boards promote a personalized support program for their missionaries. This promotes a financial and prayerful teamwork relationship between the church and its missionary. The church gets to know its missionary personally before it supports him. The missionary either is a member of the church or he ministers in the church for a time in order to develop this possible teamwork relationship on a personal basis. The church that personally knows its missionary will pray for him and financially support him. This allows the missionary the joy of reporting back to his supporting church of God's blessing and minister to them.

What is deputation and why do mission boards require it? Deputation refers to the ministry the missionary has to local churches during the time he is seeking his prayer and financial support base in order to serve on his mission field. The missionary sees himself as a servant to his churches with a desire to challenge the people of the churches to a greater involvement in and obedience to God's Great Commission of Matthew 28:16-20.

More than a "necessity," deputation is God's pattern for promoting missions in the local church, as we have seen in our Bible study of the New Testament pattern for missions. When the missionary has established a teamwork relationship with a local church, he becomes more than just a servant. At that point he becomes a staff member with an overseas or specialized area ministry.

What should a missionary candidate look for in a

mission board? The missionary should be in agreement with his mission board on their theological beliefs, with all financial policies of the mission society, and in the leadership and ministry goals.

It is wise to understand who will be in charge. To whom the missionary will be directly accountable. What form of government do the missionaries use in working together on the field? What goals the missionary will be working towards in his particular type of ministry? Will church development be the major thrust of his endeavors? Will mass evangelism be the main method to be used? Will the main work be with literature, or schools, or seminaries, or camps, or campus work, or personal evangelism, or theological education by extension, or something else?

The relationship of the mission board to a missionary family can best be illustrated by the following story of Mike, a potential missionary.

I grew up in a Christian home, but it hadn't always been so. There was a day when my Dad earned his living as an engineer. It was in those days that I seemed to lack for nothing...at least material things.

But, so many times I longed for not only a house full of "things," but also a house full of love and understanding. My Dad gave me everything I wanted, or at least that's what it seemed like, but I knew my home needed "something else."

Then it happened. A pastor came calling one day just because our family had visited the pastor's church one Easter Sunday. During that visit my Mom, Dad, younger sister and I heard how God loved us and had given His Son for us. We all trusted Christ as our personal Saviour.

What a change came over our family! Real love replaced jealousy and bickering. Dad found it a joy to be with his family, instead of spending his evenings "out with the boys." God gave meaning to each life and real purpose to us as a family. We began to pray together. That following summer my Dad made a major decision. He gave up his job as an engineer and the whole family left for another city so he could attend seminary. God had directed us to become missionaries! Dad told us it wasn't going to be easy to make this change. He would have to work twice as hard in order to study and support our family. Mom said she would have to study some, too. The Mission Board brochure we sent for said wives needed a minimum of 30 semester hours of Bible and Bible related subjects.

Dad had to enroll in the Master of Divinity program. The Mission wants well-trained workers who can be good testimonies for Christ in another culture. Dad says that sometimes American missionaries make real fools of themselves and the Lord's Name because they haven't learned well how to share Christ with a national in his country without offending him and his ways. Dad explained that some countries call us the "Ugly Americans" because we have insulted them. Therefore, Dad wanted to be the best trained and best prepared missionary possible.

Wow! Three years at seminary is a long time. Sometimes Dad worked all afternoon and late into the evening at his job after spending all morning in class. His first class at 7:30 for three years was New Testament Greek. Dad had memorization cards hanging all over the house, even on the edges of the bathroom mirror to look at while he shaved! Knowing Greek gave Dad real confidence for being able to teach the Bible. Sometimes at family devotions he would give us a Greek word that held some neat spiritual truth. He'd explain it and get us all excited because he found a new thing God was teaching him. Boy, I sure am proud of my Dad. He can really teach the Bible!

Mom was working hard, too. While Dad was studying until late at night and keeping an eye on my sis and me, Mom was taking evening classes at a nearby Bible school. Besides that, she would type all of Dad's seminary papers. Dad used to kid about supporting the local typing paper company with all the typing paper he had to buy!

With both Mom and Dad studying, there were more responsibilities for Sis and me. I really didn't mind, though, because I knew that what we were doing wasn't just a job ... we were a team working together for God.

Dad said we were preparing ourselves to be messengers of the King. We were going to carry the world's most important message from the King of Kings to people who would die without Christ if they couldn't hear the message. What a privilege!

Two important days were fast approaching: one was graduation day from seminary and the other was the day when Dad and Mom would meet with the Regional Review Committee from the Mission Board.

Just three months before, Dad and Mom had filled out an application form for the Mission Board. They wrote out their testimonies, told what they "believed" about God (Dad called it a Doctrinal Belief Statement) and gave the Mission names of people who knew them and could give references about them—and us as a family. After a couple of months the Mission sent a letter saying our references had all responded and they were setting a date for the Regional Interview. Dad was told that if the Regional Committee passed us, then we would be recommended to the Candidate Committee, which meets during the Annual Board Meetings at the Mission headquarters. Then—if we passed the Candidate Committee we would be reviewed by the entire Board of 28 men and women! It all sounded scary to me, but Mom said she was more excited than nervous.

I didn't get to be with Dad and Mom at the review meeting, but the week before the meeting the Regional Representative of the Mission stopped by the house to meet Sis and me. Mom invited him to dinner. We had a great time. He played Monopoly with us after dinner and told us to call him "Uncle Ted." He said all children in the Mission family call other missionary Moms and Dads "Aunt" and "Uncle."

We asked "Uncle Ted" lots of questions about missionary life overseas. He answered all our questions and told us about some good books we needed to read that would help us be better "junior missionaries."

Mom and Dad, along with Sis and me, went to McDonald's to celebrate! We had been recommended to the next level of the Mission Board for appointment as missionaries. Our pastor and his wife went with us to have a hamburger and a milk shake. Pastor told Dad that the whole church has been praying for us and that if we were appointed they would help support us to get us out to the field as quickly as possible. (Our pastor happens to be a member of the Mission Board.) He assured us that other churches would want to help us, too. He said that's their way of obeying the Lord's Great Commission.

I know there's no way I can convince you how excited I am about being part of a missionary team. I'm sure it sounds silly, but I feel I'm following the pattern we see in the Bible of Paul, Silas, Barnabas and Timothy. They, along with others, like Dr. Luke and Peter, were the team God put together for sharing Christ to their generation. I want to be part of a team to do the same thing in my generation, even as a "missionary kid"! My teammates are all part of my Mission Society *and* all the people of the local churches that support us. That's quite a team. For me, it's God's team.

By now I trust we can see the necessity of a teamwork relationship between the church, mission board and the missionary. These are some of the things that need to be determined as the missionary candidate looks for just the right "team" to serve with to the glory of God.

CHAPTER 9

The Effective Twentieth Century Missionary

Marjorie Shelley

Hmmm click. "This is our hut."

Hmmm click. "This is our boat."

Hmmm click. "This is our guide."

On and on (and on and on) it goes. The missionary's slide show. One of those all-time favorites, rating right up there with a trip to the dentist.

Finally, mercifully, the slides end. Everyone sings two verses of "I'll Go Where You Want Me to Go." The pastor asks all the young people to raise their hands if they're ready to dedicate themselves to "full-time Christian work." Then a benediction. And then we escape . . . er . . . "go our separate ways."

Sad, isn't it?

Especially when that's the only impression most people get of what a missionary's life is all about. It comes across as an ordeal. Something to be endured.

Let me try to smash some of those stereotypes for you. You see, if being a missionary was as bad as some of the slide shows I've seen, it would be fit only for masochists. But it's not. I know. I'm a missionary. And, believe it or not, I enjoy my job.

Unfortunately, people in churches back home still have a warped view of us, our personalities, and our job description. Some of the cliches I hear when I'm in the States make me squirm!

"Tonight we have a real live missionary!" (I've always wanted to snarl, bare my teeth, and shake my furry mane to prove I'm "really alive.")

"She's been over in dark Africa winning the heathen to Christ." (I'm much more afraid of the heathen in New York subways.)

"Here is Marjorie Missionary to present the challenge of the mission field." As if only those who travel to another continent can talk about Christ. I'd much rather be "Marj Shelley who tells her friends about her Other Friend, Jesus Christ.")

I wince. The audience yawns. And out float all the images of nineteenth century colonialism—sun helmets, mosquito-veils, dumpy clothes, racism, snake skins, and hair pulled up in a bun.

The problem with that stereotype (like most stereotypes) is that most missionaries don't fit it. Some do. Most don't. Just like a few athletes give all "dumb jocks" a bad name, a few provincial missionaries can cause problems for all the others.

The missionaries I know aren't losers sent to Africa because they couldn't get along with anyone in their native country. They aren't social outcasts or misfits.

Who is, then, the effective twentieth century missionary? How can you tell a good one from a bad one?

Above all, he (or she) is one who recognizes that he lives in the last quarter of the twentieth century. It's time to shuck outmoded concepts and level with ourselves. Overseas governments, industries, and churches are facing twentieth century problems. They have no time for foreigners who haven't adapted to the times.

Three Important Changes

From a long list of indicators, I have chosen three to highlight the changes foreign missionaries have had to adjust to in the past 25 years.

The Rush to the Cities. Everywhere in the world, masses of people are leaving rural areas and flooding into the cities. As Roger S. Greenway writes in an article titled, "Mission to an Urban World" (*Church Growth Bulletin,* September 1975), "In the year 1800, three percent of the world lived in cities. By 1900 the number had risen to 13 percent. It is predicted that by the year 2000, 87 percent of the world's population will be located in urban centers." The missionary wearing a pith helmet and driving a Land Rover into the bush is gradually becoming extinct. Most sending agencies for missionaries are having to change their strategy.

Education and Professionalism. In the days of Hudson Taylor (in the 1760s), the China Inland Mission was opened to those of "little formal education." Yet, in 1974 an African Christian stood before church leaders and said, "The day when it was enough to send us missionaries with only a Bible school education is finished. We want to work with missionaries who are scholastically qualified to train our people." In countries which pour 35 per cent of their national budget into educational programs, only well-trained missionaries are accepted.

Missionaries must be more than sincere, well-meaning folk telling primitive tribesmen about the Great White-Man's God. Today's missionaries must be sincere, well-meaning professionals.

Missions is changing from its flannelgraph-in-the-grass-hut image. Missionaries now must be well-trained (hopefully with at least a Master's degree). They are doctors, nurses, journalists, editors, business managers, engineers, artists, recreation directors, and countless other specific professions. All require special training.

No longer should you settle for an "I'm a missionary" statement from someone. Ask them for specifics. What's their job?

"I'm a photographer for a magazine," or "I'm a pastor" gives you a much better idea of what they really do. It'll help you pray for them more knowledgeably in their own unique ministry.

Working Under the National Christians. In today's third world countries, Christians are sensitive about having foreigners running their churches. The church is God's instrument for bringing in and maturing new Christians. Attitudes of superiority, racism, and bigotry by even one missionary can wipe out the ministry of an entire mission.

Thus, missionaries are wanted only if they will serve under the national church leaders, and if they are effective serving that way.

Nationals want to develop their own churches in their own ways. When a local church leader told a missionary not to do evangelism without an African, the missionary asked for the church to supply the men. None were offered. Another missionary asked, "Would the church prefer no evangelism rather than allowing a white man to do it?" The answer was: "Peut-etre." (Perhaps.)

Twentieth century missionaries must recognize that unless they work with (and under) the local Christians, they can do more harm to God's work than good.

What Kind of Person Is Needed?

What kind of person should the twentieth century missionary be?

A flexible person. "Be a missionary? I couldn't stand the bugs and snakes!" Who can? Most women missionaries—single or married— would say the same thing.

While it is true a missionary must physically and mentally adjust to strange insects, heat, malaria, dysentery, dust, water shortages, no electricity, these minor irritations often seem just that—minor.

But the missionary must be most adaptable in the realm of interpersonal relationships. As he travels from church to church in his homeland he is showered with gifts, love, friendship, and encouragement. He arrives on the field to learn he is no hero to the nationals. In fact, one of the first questions may be: "Why are *you* here?" What a comedown!

At the hour for quitting time, a nurse in a maternity ward asked an African colleague, "Could you stay with this woman for thirty minutes while I have supper? Then I'll spend the night."

"Huh? You can stay," was the answer. "That's why you came. Don't you want to serve our people?"

Some young missionaries are hurt because they never receive thanks for what they do. Some who work among Muslims have tried to show the love of Christ caring for sick people, helping the women, repairing motorbikes for the men—utterly giving of themselves—only to hear, "Oh, he was just trying to gain favor with his God."

Whether it is as fraternal workers with the church or under the church, the twentieth century missionary now takes orders.

"Oh, I wouldn't have any problem there," some may say.

"Really? And what if the standards of the church are lowered, sin is tolerated and condoned, evangelism drops off, money becomes a major issue? The missionary who makes it is the one who patiently prays, teaches, counsels, and tactfully serves.

A humble person. When the local policeman unjustly accuses a missionary of breaking the law, and the missionary realizes it is because his skin is the wrong color, what should he do? The backlash of colonialism still has its effects and the best way to cope is to smile and take it. A reluctance to work under national leadership, a failure to accept criticism from the nationals, or a paternalistic hangover from the "old days" will lead to unhappiness and ineffectiveness. The missionary needs to be a humble person.

An emotionally stable person. There are separations and loneliness. Can he cope with these? The emotional leaving of family and friends is one of the hardest things missionaries of any century face. This is just something which must be endured. Perhaps this is only the beginning of hardship, yet none of the sufferings can make one give up if he is sure he is in the hand of God.

Are single women the only missionaries who suffer loneliness? No, missionary wives—and yes, even the men—must make this emotional adjustment.

How would the problem arise? In many ways.

- A young mother never gets the chance to learn the language well. Her husband, very busy with evangelism tours, or working in the radio studio or production office, does not see what is happening as she grows more lonely and more depressed.

- A single woman, frightened and lonely, has never really faced the issue of remaining single all her life. She becomes depressed, misses her family and friends, and slowly shuts out the rest of the world.

- The young missionary man feels completely frustrated while standing alone in the face of an independent national church which has lost its zeal, or permits adultery in its ranks, or fails to give for the Lord's work.

- A young widow returns home to an empty house, misses her children far away in school, and aches for someone with whom to share her feelings.

Though loneliness is not unique to the mission field, it does become more acute there. There is no warm church family in which to lose oneself. Christmas and Easter, which seem uniquely family occasions, become more painful. Recreation and distractions must be created. The missionary advisor to the local church has no other pastors to consult. He is always "the foreigner."

Will anything help to strengthen the missionary emotionally? Yes. Face facts before leaving home. Remember to see the humorous sides of most things. Bounce back from the roughest blows. All these will help. And remember that you can do anything through the help of Christ, as the Apostle Paul, that greatest of missionaries, said: "I know both how to be abased, and I know how to abound: every where and in all things I am instructed both to be full and to be hungry, both to abound and to suffer need. I can do all things through Christ which strengtheneth me" (Philippians 4:12,13).

One who is free of anxieties. I knew of a missionary wife who could not adjust to living in a foreign country. Fear of infections, microbes and disease drove her to fanatically seek measures against them. She and her husband were gradually forced to resign.

Fear of entrusting one's children to houseparents hundreds of miles away has gnawed at the hearts of some parents.

Anxieties over the future can drain the enthusiasm for

foreign service. Will I have a retirement fund built up? If this country closes to missionaries, will I be able to learn another language? Perhaps such fears and anxieties are normal. But, should they be normal for Christian workers?

Missions have changed as societies have changed. Modes and methods change. But, the Christ who calls is unchangeable. The twentieth century missionary must set his mind and heart to face circumstances realizing that Christ will help him to meet each situation.

Can he be spiritually prepared? An African proverb says: "Two chiefs cannot row in the same canoe." That seems the answer to any queries about the twentieth century missionary. If Christ is chief in the canoe, a person can row overseas or anywhere else with confidence. If self becomes chief and takes first place, doubts, anxieties, loneliness, all mushroom.

Before boarding the plane for overseas duty, a young person should settle it with the Lord: "Lord, here I am. Whatever I am and have are Yours. I can't make it by myself. I'm putting everything in Your hands. I want Christ to have full control."

That is really what Romans 12:1 and 2 is all about . . . presenting your body a living sacrifice, holy, acceptable unto God. Once on the field today's missionary, like thousands who served before him, may forget this dedication. Moreover, he must constantly guard against a dried-up devotional life. Let down the guard, slip a few times, and early storm warnings appear: an angry word, impatience, emotional crises, lack of insight, failure to show Christian love.

At this low point loneliness is amplified, anxieties increase, and questions swirl in his thoughts:

"Am I really supposed to be here?"

"Have I misinterpreted God's leading?"

"Maybe I should go back? I'll never be a success as a missionary."

Amazingly enough, when we get back to God's Word and on speaking terms with Him, He handles the problems well. Oh, I don't mean it suddenly becomes easy. The missionary must still work in spite of disinterested or even hostile people. He makes mistakes and he may often ask forgiveness. Yet, through disappointments, he finds real satisfaction in allowing Christ to do the job, saying, "I am crucified with Christ: nevertheless I live; yet not I, but Christ liveth in me: and the life which I now live in the flesh I live by the faith of the Son of God, who loved me, and gave himself for me" (Galatians 2:20).

He then gains personal satisfaction as well. When the old man, after listening and finally understanding, exclaims: "Unhungh! I understand. The Jesus road is the right one!"

Or, when a national Christian says, "Thank you. You are the first white person ever to ask forgiveness. Jesus is real!"

When an African co-worker says, "I am surrounded by love. I want to work here because you love me."

Yes, when such spontaneous exclamations come, it is worth all the frustration and pain.

One realizes the twentieth century missionary has new problems, new pressures, and new means of meeting them. But, when all the analysis is done, he doesn't have any pat answers either. Yet, he can go on working that he might by all means bring some to a measure of maturity in Christ even as he himself learns of Him.

CHAPTER 10

Facing
a Different Culture

George Patterson

To enjoy living in another land the missionary must become sensitive to a new way of life. A different country means a different culture. But *who* is different?

Understanding the Differences

When you go to a foreign country as a missionary, it is you who are different! You will talk funny and walk with that odd, loose-jointed American stride. You may have a peculiar body odor that—to a Brazilian, for example—smells like wet chicken feathers.

Fitting into a new culture requires more than learning their customs. You must look at yourself as they do. You must learn what your strange ways are. What are Americans like to the rest of the world? Our individualism, democracy and independent thinking are not the normal thing. We are the odd ones. In most countries people consider us intelligent but culturally stupid; fair but loud-mouthed; generous but careless with money; curious but stubborn; honest with others but impatient; handcuffed by our wristwatch to a relentless time schedule.

Don't worry about having to change overnight. Don't try to put on an act; don't try to be what you're not. Wearing a poncho won't make you a Mexican. Riding a camel won't make you an Arab. Be yourself. But be conscious of how folks see you. Then you will avoid doing those little things that offend them (like speaking English near them, complaining about discomforts, criticizing their products and services, talking loudly and bugging them about how late they arrive at meetings).

You will be tempted to gossip with other Americans about how impossible the nationals are. How long it takes to place a telephone call! How needless their government red tape! How smelly the market place! So many thieves and beggars! Don't fall into this trap. Don't start feeling superior. You have inherited—through no merit of your own—the influence of centuries of scientific development, Christian teaching and technical progress. But had you been born and raised in their circumstances, without these advantages, you would have been just like them. Don't foreget, not too long ago our ancestors were called "barbarians."

Our Christian love for people ought to be strong enough to overlook their apparent flaws. Some missionaries forget they are guests of a foreign country. They try to change everything overnight. They expect the new Christians to dress and eat like Americans. In underdeveloped countries we may think that our superior education gives us the right to run the show. But the strongest national churches are often those where missionaries have worked the *least*. A wise missionary knows when to keep out of the way. We must let the nationals do their own work, make their own mistakes and grow in experience and wisdom.

We must also learn to *appreciate* their culture. You won't automatically like it: it takes hard study. You must discover its origins, read its literature and observe its art. Investigate its history until you find why the people act and believe as they do. Learn their laws, beliefs, hopes and fears. Are they afraid of a take-over by the United

States? By Russia? By foreign industry? What do they write about us in their papers? What kind of government do they have? Are they suspicious of big business? If so, why? What have large landowners or corporations done to them for the last few hundred years?

When we see something we don't like, we must not criticize. We should rather find out *why* it is. Then we will often appreciate and even love their differences.

Facing Culture Shock

What is culture shock? The shock comes when unexpected things pain us. Our family is hurt by a lack of understanding by the people of the other society. We feel that no one appreciates us; we can trust no one! Fortunately, these moods usually pass quickly.

Culture shock also pains us when we return to the U.S.A., after having become accustomed to the way things are normally elsewhere. The waste, the carelessness and the lack of human warmth shock us.

We are also shocked by the poverty in most countries. We see death, violence and disease everywhere. The men earn too little and eat poorly. Their children need medicine. Their women are ignorant of many simple things which would help them keep more comfortable homes. They have six to a dozen children—far too many to feed.

Poverty usually has spiritual causes. Poverty's favorite companions are superstition, idolatry, immorality and dishonesty. That is why our poverty programs always fail when we give the people only money and machines. They need to learn honesty, the need to keep contracts, to pay debts and take responsibility. They need to build spiritual foundations.

We won't help at all if we stand around wringing our hands and feeling shocked. We must get to work and study the Biblical solutions for their problems. Wherever the gospel has been proclaimed and practiced for many years, entire societies have progressed. The power of Christ breaks the grip of Satan on the minds of people long given to idols, opium, booze and immorality.

Poverty causes selfishness and dishonesty. Selfishness and dishonesty cause more poverty. This vicious circle yields when we proclaim Christ, educate the people and help them to help themselves.

The apparent injustice in some societies also shocks us. We see the very rich living beside the very poor without taking any notice of them. We find caste systems and mistreatment of the lower classes. Unbridled prejudice! People are thrown in jail for any accusation. There is no public trial; a man is tortured until he confesses. Release from prison depends on friends and money. Companies pay their workers only a dollar a day to support their large families. Men engender dozens of babies whom they never support.

We may be shocked to find there are no real free elections; the government is unstable. You may have to spend tiresome hours in several hot, crowded offices to get one necessary document. The officials may snap at you. Your individual rights are overlooked. You will need patience. Remember, American democracy is not the only kind of government, even among the "free" nations. We must not criticize the other governments. People will resent it (they may criticize their own government bitterly; but won't let a foreigner do it). We had better stay out of their politics. We should study the reasons why their government is as it is. The people often want the kind of government they have, even though they complain about it.

Social injustice, class discrimination and government corruption abound in the United States, too. Only we keep them better hidden. We become blind to our own faults. Many a foreigner, however, is shocked by what he finds in the U.S.

The best remedy for culture shock is to *cultivate close fellowship with the Lord Jesus Christ.* He is the Universal Man: He fits into any culture. He helps us forget our prejudices. His love and peace give us the patience and humility to forget our selfish ideas and to understand unsympathetic people.

Understanding people who dislike us requires a lot of grace. You go to a village to win the people for Christ. You love them. You are concerned for their salvation; you feel the pain of their poverty; you go to help them. You pay a lot of money to get there but it's worth it, you say. Your car gets stuck in a sand bank crossing a river on the way. But you walk on, expecting your reward in grateful souls. But no one comes to listen to you. An old woman and some children come to hear you preach and laugh at you. Some young men throw rocks and break your new Coleman lamp. As you leave the village you hear them jeering and hooting.

You try to tell yourself to be cheerful but it's too hot. The dust in the road chokes you every time a horse gallops by. Your legs itch from a hundred tick bites. You are sweaty and there is nowhere to bathe. You arrive at home and find that someone has stolen your front gate, right off its hinges. You start to go to bed but there is an urgent problem in one of the churches. A worker is waiting to talk to you. It won't wait, he says, and they're blaming you for the whole thing.

You will either accept the whole experience with a sense of humor or feel sorry for yourself. Feeling sorry for yourself is an early symptom of that fatal strain of culture shock which sooner or later sends its victim back to the States. Get over it quickly! Don't feel sorry for yourself, no matter what they do or say. It'll eat on you until folks can see the bitterness in your face.

A second remedy for culture shock is to *maintain a normal family life.* Some missionaries spend all their time in the work. When they are at home they always have visitors or are typing reports. Their children do not enjoy happy moments when their parents show their interest in them and give them their time without complaining. You will need to spend time together as a family—just your family. Never forget this. Family problems are the number one cause on the missionary casualty list. We can take a lot of criticism and defeats as long as we have a peaceful refuge to retire to: a home where love, joy and confidence reign.

Another remedy for culture shock is to *brace yourself for the blow.* Find out before you go something about what it's going to be like. What kind of bugs will you have in your bedroom? How much does it rain? How hot is it? What will you eat? Are there roads or will you have to walk to your churches? Can you travel by mule, canoe or by air? Ask returned missionaries how people dress, how they live and what their greatest problems are. Visit another country if you can. Go as a tourist or on a summer service project. It will open your mind, no matter what country you live in. You will learn to adapt and to control your prejudices.

A young person interested in missions should start reading about other cultures. Don't be satisfied just to learn their interesting differences. Find out why they are different. Never stop investigating until you have discovered why the people do things in a "different" way. Why do the men in Guatemalan villages wear skirts? Why do the Hindus worship cows? Why do they hang on to the caste system? What are its strengths, to have lasted for so many centuries? Why do the people of Central America eat beans three times a day? Why the thatched roofs and dirt floors? Consult one or more librarians about your interest. They could recommend good books or guide you in a helpful project for better understanding.

Cross-Cultural Communication

You won't be long in a foreign country before you find how easy it is to be misunderstood. You may pronounce the right words correctly but your ideas just don't come across. Communication requires more than words. Our words carry meaning only when we relate them to ideas. Our minds hold millions of memories, ideas, facts and feelings. Our words transmit thoughts accurately only to persons whose minds also contain similar memories, ideas, facts and feelings. Persons in dissimilar societies also have a great store of memories and ideas. But theirs are quite different from ours. Our words, even translated correctly, fail to call forth the same ideas. We will not arrive at the same conclusions. People out of politeness will agree with us and seem to appreciate what we are saying, but later we discover that our words left impressions which we never intended.

People in some rural, non-industrial societies do not think in language symbols as much as we do. They do not reason in terms of logical cause and effect or proofs and conclusions supported by clear evidence. They think in terms of animals, plants, weather, nature and human relationships. Their thinking is visual and emotional; their ideas are images of those things which they see or do. They read little and care little for abstract thoughts. Their conversation is frank and direct, flavored with strong feelings.

In other societies communication is indirect. In Japan you cannot just sit down with a friend and come to the point of something you care to discuss or communicate.

You have to reach it by an indirect route, traveling around the subject at a distance, drinking tea, until you finally zero it in. The people love abstraction. In India among some castes you would not show emotion in your conversation even though they were cutting off your thumbs.

Within the same country you may find cultures so different that the people cannot understand each other, even though they speak the same language. In Honduras an educated pastor in a city church often finds it impossible to pastor the uneducated villagers from the interior. The social classes are so separated by different ideas and values that a pastor must be of the same class of people as his congregation. Churches which mix the city and mountain people with their opposing mentalities suffer continual quarrels. Such cultural differences make greater barriers to communication than language differences.

In some villages, even though a person arrives late for the worship service, he greets everyone when he enters. The speaker may spit on the floor; dogs or pigs wander about freely; a woman will sing a special number holding a child to her breast. When these people come to the city, the rigid formality in the church discourages them. They feel left out of it. They misunderstand the logical, analytical reasoning of the pastor. They think he's showing off (especially when he wears a coat and tie). The separate ways of thinking of the two sub-cultures have roots too deep to reconcile their differences easily. The educated class looks down on the villagers, who accept their inferior status without a murmur. If you urge them to fight for their rights they shake their heads, feeling sorry for your lack of understanding. "Rights? Don't you know that we were *born* to be poor and ignorant? Nothing can change *that!*"

We must carry the gospel from one country to another and from one culture to another within a country. How can this vital message cross these cultural barriers? There is a very Biblical solution. It is so simple that many missionaries miss it. They are seeking some sophisticated key to cross-culture communication. *The simple solution is to teach at first only the bare, essential gospel, which can be understood in any culture.* In other words, peel off all non-essentials and plant only the bare seed of the gospel.

Later, let the natives add their own customs, rituals and ideas to it. The new churches do not need to inherit our rituals and customs. *So what* if they don't have any "pulpit?" So what if they meet at night instead of Sunday morning for their main worship service? So what if it lasts three hours? So what if they don't give a public invitation to *go forward* to accept Christ? So what if their hymns use melodies that hurt our ears? So what if they don't divide their families into age groups for a "Sunday School?" So what if a toothless old woman sings her special number off key and changes the words as she goes along? So what if a family arrives at church for the first time and announces that they are now Christians, just like that, without having ever attended an evangelistic service? So what if the pews have no backs? So what if the men and women sit on opposite sides? So what if they refuse to turn their backsides toward the altar when they kneel to pray? So what if they do not hold annual elections with a secret ballot? So what if they don't have one pastor who does all the preaching? So what if they serve each person a large glass for the Lord's Supper and sip it very slowly? So what if they prefer experience-related Bible studies geared to their needs instead of our systematic lessons? So what if the deacons serve the Lord's Supper dressed only in loin cloths? These external things, and a hundred more, are only the wrapping in which men present the gospel of Christ.

Suppose, for example, that we send a gift to a tribe in the jungle. It may be a precious jewel or a New Testament, recently translated into their dialect. It may be vaccine to stop an epidemic. We pack it in a metal box to keep out the tropical moisture, and bind it with metal straps, to protect it. But the tribesmen do not have the proper tools to open the package. They do not even know it's supposed to be opened. It is so prettily wrapped; that's all they see. They like it. They mount it on a thirty foot pole in the village square and worship it. They praise its beauty and the strength of its wrappings. *That* is what we often do with the gospel. We wrap it in American customs and ways of thinking. We protect it from corruption so well that the people never really find it for themselves.

We must strip the gospel of all our customs and safeguards and entrust it to the nationals in its pure, original form. The announcement of repentance and forgiveness of sin in the name of Jesus Christ is *the* New Testament message: the key, promised first to Peter, to open the door of God's kingdom to the believing sinner. We should ask nothing from our new churches except obedience to the commands of Christ. This is the Great Commission of Matthew 28:18-20; we are to make disciples by teaching them to do all the things that Christ commanded. What are His commands for His churches?

Let us learn the things He has ordered us to do. To receive God's forgiveness in Christ, we must renounce our sin and believe in Him. Then, we learn to observe the rest of His commands: we are baptized; we love God and men in a practical way; we celebrate the Lord's Supper in fellowship with other believers; we pray; we confess Jesus Christ as our Lord before the world; we give and live an unselfish, useful life, separated from sin. These, then, are the bare essentials: the key to unlock the door in the most difficult culture. How simple! Keep it that simple and it is that easy.

We must let a new group of believers in a different culture begin by doing these basic, essential things ordered by the Lord. Then they *are* a church. Afterwards, they can shape their own evangelical traditions and develop their own liturgy. Liturgy means the methods of worship of any church. The national churches study the Word of God to apply it in their own way to their own culture.

The Word of God is universal. We Americans have interpreted it from within our own narrow cultural context. Few Americans realize how very narrow our ideas are. The most liberal-minded among us are often the narrowest when it comes to accepting the ideas of other societies. We must give the nationals the right to interpret the Word from within their own cultural context, just as we have done. They will be narrow, too. We must put up with ideas which we don't like.

The Great Commission requires us to make disciples who obey Christ's commandments for His churches. This is where we must start, in a foreign land, not by translating fat textbooks or building Bible schools or founding tiny American colonies. In order to make obedient disciples of Christ we first distinguish between three levels of authority for His churches. They are: *Divine commandments, apostolic practices* and *human customs.* Each has a certain authority:

1. DIVINE COMMANDMENTS (We must obey them, by order of our Lord: Matthew 28:18-20.)
2. APOSTOLIC PRACTICES (Things which New Testament churches did but were never commanded: we have no authority to command them nor to pro-

hibit them—only Christ has this authority over His churches.)

3. HUMAN CUSTOMS (Evangelical practices not mentioned in the New Testament: we cannot command them; we may prohibit them if they impede obedience. God recognizes their validity only on the basis of the voluntary agreement of a certain congregation to follow them: Matthew 18:18-20.)

Most cross-culture communication problems disappear when our churches clarify these three levels of authority. Let us consider examples of these three levels.

God's commandments must be obeyed; Christ Himself ordered these things as part of His New Testament. Only He has the authority to say what His churches must do (Matthew 28:18). It is a *commandment,* for example, to baptize new believers. To baptize them immediately was an *apostolic practice* (not to be made obligatory nor to be prohibited when circumstances warrant following the apostles' example). To baptize only after a long course of doctrine is a *human custom,* whose only authority, according to Christ, lies in a congregation's voluntary agreement to do it.

Repentance from sin is a *commandment.* To express this repentance by "praying through," "going forward in front of a crowd," weeping at the altar or doing acts of penance, are all *human customs.* A convert's sincerity in doing any of these customs depends on his background. For us, acts of penance may reflect only hypocrisy. For other peoples, they may be done in deep conviction of the Holy Spirit, out of heartfelt repentance. For this reason we must never judge the customs of another congregation, only our own. We are responsible to God for what *we* do. The worst thing we could do is translate from English our books on church policy, for the developing congregations.

Cross-cultural communication of the gospel requires

peeling off all human customs and planting the bare seed
of the New Testament proclamation and commands of
Christ. If we communicate these basic truths in love, the
one universal language, the new church certainly will
grow. Then we must let the nationals' congregations
develop their own customs. Some of them we will not like.
So in Christian humility we will keep our mouth shut.

Presenting Christ in Another Culture

How do men make sincere decisions in faith? What kind
of decision for Christ is really sealed by the Holy Spirit? In
America the democratic spirit has taught us from infancy
that a true decision is made by the individual who stands
alone, on his own two feet, before his God, with no
influence from family or friends. In the American culture
this is often the way we make sincere decisions; the Holy
Spirit blesses such a decision. But not so in most other
societies. Our way of making decisions is completely
foreign to most other peoples. Going forward during a
public invitation appeals to the individual to step out from
his friends and family and stand alone for Christ. Only a
small percentage of persons who receive Christ this way
in Latin America show any evidence afterward of being
born again.

So what kind of decision does the Holy Spirit seal in the
heart of a typical non-American? A person in most
cultures makes sincere decisions only after having an
understanding with his family and friends. He cannot
receive Christ alone, without letting them know his
intentions and talking about it: such a lone decision is not
culturally sound; it is not sincere. We see entire families
making decisions together in the Bible. Lydia, the seller of
purple, received Christ with her family. The Philippian
jailer and Crispus, the ruler of the Corinthian synagogue,
also received Christ with their entire families. When

Peter preached Christ in Cornelius the Centurion's house, everyone present was converted. Why? They did not invite the public to that meeting. Cornelius invited only his family members and close friends (Acts 10:24). This does not mean that a family or group has to make a unified decision, all together. It means that the individual must clear his conscience with the rest of his social group or family, and declare his intentions, before his decision for Christ can be sincere. He cannot make it alone. He may be the only one of the group to decide at first, but the rest will know it and will often follow him—if the American missionary keeps his individualistic thinking out of the way. Decisions made this way in Latin America almost always yield evidence of being born again.

Evangelists are harvesters. If an American harvesting method results in only 5 per cent follow-through in another land, we had better examine what we are doing. The more Biblical, historically proven harvesting method, of making decisions voluntarily through the influence of family and friends, often results in 95 per cent follow-through. How many farmers would keep a harvesting machine which collected 95 per cent waste and weeds? To whom could he sell his grain? The American missionary must root out cherished ideas from his own mind, painful as it will be. He must recognize how people will receive Christ in the new culture where he will work.

Another difference in the way people receive Christ as Saviour lies in what actually convinces them. In America the Holy Spirit usually uses a doctrinal, logical argument to convince the doubter. But in Spanish America the sinner already believes; the Holy Spirit uses a loving call to repentance from sin to convict him. In Brazil the Holy Spirit often convinces the seeker with a Biblical answer to his preoccupation with death. In Russia many are convinced by an appeal to the justice of the Christian ethic. Americans waste time witnessing to these people with doctrinal arguments and logical one-two-three-four presentations of the "plan of salvation." That's not what they need. They aren't fighting the intellectual side of Christian theology. The devil has them hung up on another issue.

How can a missionary ever make so many adaptations? How can we change our thoughts so radically? We have a hidden weapon, an aid, which diplomats and international salesmen lack, for adapting to foreign cultures. Missionaries have always fitted into different societies easier than unbelieving traders and diplomats living in foreign capitals. Jesus Christ is inside of us. He is the Universal Man. He fits into all cultures, because God made all men with just that purpose: to have them become conformed to the image of His Son. Christ attracts Hindu, Moslem, Jew, Communist and Indian alike—when He is presented as He is, and not clothed in blue jeans with a tag saying "Made in USA." Jesus Christ is the common denominator, the bridge between all cultures, the one who has broken down the wall of enmity between Jew and Gentile and all other races. Take Him with you into a foreign port, along with your passport and vaccination papers; you will be surprised how He helps you get along.

CHAPTER 11

Overcoming Hindrances to Service

Lois Morden

The most wonderful "job" that is offered to young people today is serving the Lord, and we as missionaries could even narrow that down a bit and say serving on the mission field. However, with all the blessings, joys, opportunities and rewards that come there are hindrances that could either keep us from going to the field or send us home disappointed to seek another type of service. I would like to speak rather frankly about some of the hindrances that Satan might try to use to keep one from fulfilling God's perfect will for his life.

Hindrances in Deputation

Feeling "On Exhibit." When a missionary goes into a church on deputation he feels that he is on exhibit. He knows that people are watching and that he's being appraised by everyone. If his wife wears makeup, ear rings, and nail polish, she's apt to be called vain or worldly. If she's lacking the fancy "do-dads," she's drab and really looks like a missionary. If he is well dressed, he's extravagant. If he's still wearing last furlough's suit, he's tacky and outdated.

When sometimes the entire family is involved, special care is taken when the family is dressing to select just the right clothes. The children are primed on how to act, but they resent the fact that they can't be just normal kids. The resent being "part of the exhibit."

One church requested that our children accompany us and participate in the Sunday services. When the children were told this, it was like waving a red flag in front of a bull. They got all "fussed up" and "snorted" and couldn't understand why they had to go. Well, Mom and Dad prayed much about it but when the day arrived it was anything but easy to get those two willful teenagers on the move. We left with a prayer on our lips to the Lord to remove the scowls, the grumps and the rebellion.

On the way home, after a very successful day, we thanked the children for their friendliness with the people and their cooperation in the presentation. Our daughter remarked, "I don't know why, I had made up my mind that I wasn't going to cooperate, but I just had to." That brought forth a prayer of thankfulness to the Lord who had marvelously come to our rescue and changed discontent to joy, and rebellion to cooperation.

A letter was later received with words of commendation and appreciation to the children for their presence and participation. It turned out to be a delightful experience, but imagine what might have happened had the Lord not been asked to intervene!

Yes, the missionary is always "on exhibit" and resentment of this fact can be a hindrance to good attitudes toward deputation. A missionary must do his best to be the attractive person that God would have him to be, in manner of dress, in grooming, and in relationships with His children. To God we are always on exhibit. He sees our every action, reads our every thought, and knows our every desire. If God is pleased with our appearance and our actions, we have passed the test. Even though the missionary is "on exhibit" before the people and subject to their criticism, he can have poise and complete confidence if he has his Heavenly Father's approval.

Fearing New Contacts. Deputation means visiting churches and meeting people. Do you enjoy meeting new people? Many missionaries really don't. Some are naturally timid persons and have to make themselves talk to strangers. A missionary has to raise his own support and that means that he must visit churches and show himself friendly. Who would ever support an antisocial missionary? People like missionaries to be outgoing—to have a good platform manner and to be at ease in the presence of others. They have to be able to present their field of service in a challenging way so that the people will want to give to their support. How can a shy person ever visit churches on deputation, continually meet new people and try to interest them in supporting him on the mission field?

Let us consider the answer to these questions. Who made us? God did! Who calls us to be missionaries? God does! Does God give all those whom He calls an outgoing personality so that they find it easy to meet new people and make them friends? Certainly not! God made some of us the shy persons that we are and that for a very good reason. He loves variety and shows it in the marvelous creations that are all around us. He is a great lover of colors, of different sizes and shapes, and of innumerable characteristics that our little minds can hardly fathom. When He looked upon His creation He saw that it was GOOD! To each of us, as the crown of His creation, He has given a personality that pleases Him, and shyness may be a part of that gift. Just because we may fear new contacts that doesn't mean we can't successfully meet new people. It will be harder for us, but the "all things" of Philippians

4:13 is our special promise.

A few years ago we were furloughing at the time of the annual meetings of our mission society and I was asked to speak for five minutes during a banquet served in a large dining room in the Conrad-Hilton Hotel in Chicago. Just the thought of it sent my stomach into convulsions. I couldn't! Whatever could I say to all those people? Why did they ask me? These thoughts and others raced through my perturbed brain and my reaction was that it was simply impossible. Fortunately, I stopped to think and I remembered that my Father made me the way I am and He also was responsible for this seemingly impossible request. He is strength, wisdom, friendliness, and all the rest rolled up into one and He was ready, willing, and even desiring to use me to fulfill this appointment. With His assurance echoing in my heart, I was made able to do the job that He had given me. The butterflies wouldn't permit me to eat of the sumptuous fare so beautifully served, but my mission was accomplished in His power and for His glory.

Deputation can be successful only in this way. One doesn't have to be a fireball personality to attract and challenge, but one does have to be a simple instrument in the hands of a Mighty God. He is our omniscient Friend and He can enable us to meet others. He can use us—weak, shy, incapable persons that we may be—to be a blessing and a challenge. Deputation can be successful because of His enabling.

Resenting Extraordinary Demands. One thing that a missionary learns as an appointee is that he can do anything: perform the humble tasks of a servant, be the teacher of ANY age group, be the counselor for upset marriages, or the visitor of delinquent members. It is good for him to know this as he begins to tackle deputation appointments and accept it as truth for it will help him to preserve his ordinarily "sweet" disposition. Of course, we all have those two natures squabbling within us and sometimes the wrong one shows his teeth and the missionary falls from his "pedestal." Maybe he thinks he had reason when he balked and unthinkingly said, "I don't know what some pastors think we are!" This reminds me of one of my husband's experiences.

It was camp time and missionaries are indispensable at camps. Usually their responsibilities are limited to presenting a missionary challenge to the young people and counseling them along these lines. However, one camp director decided that the boys really needed to get to know their missionary. What better way is there than to have a missionary camp out with a different group of boys each night? Sounds like a wonderful idea!

The missionary and another counselor were to take a group out in the afternoon, cook their evening meal over an open fire, have a time of devotions with them and then help them get settled down for sleeping out under the stars (except when it rained). Frying eggs for breakfast for the hungry mob was part of the plan and the boys thought that it was absolutely GREAT. Each group was more enthusiastic than the previous one, and everyone thought it was such a success that it should be a regular part of the program.

How does the missionary fare in all of this? He's a bit on the low side physically after four years in a tropical country, working under continual pressures and being inflicted with malaria and intestinal parasites. Instead of being able to enjoy a bit of comfort, he is obliged to pass sleepless nights with his old friends, the mosquitos, and to relish the bonfire meals that his unaccustomed hands must prepare. After all, he is the missionary and is used to outdoor hardships, so what better person could successfully do the job?

Now, how is the missionary going to react? Is the old nature going to show his fangs? He probably has reason as the request certainly is a bit out of the ordinary and would bring out the worst in anyone. However, the child of God is also blessed with a new nature that knows how to be submissive to authority, to act in love instead of reacting in resentment. Even though he might suffer physically, a right attitude might just turn some young person on for missions, and if so, the job can be considered "well done, good and faithful servant." Extraordinary demands come to all and we as missionaries are responsible—not to the pastor or the camp director—but to the Lord Himself, our Authority, as to how we react to them.

Begging for Support. Some have said, "I can't go out and beg for support to go to the mission field. Why can't the mission just have a pooled fund and support those who apply from those funds?" Probably all of us have had those feelings at one time or another. It is difficult to go out and raise your own support. Whenever there is an increase in salary, the missionary has to ask his supporters for additional funds or seek to enlist others to give. Will you be able to do this?

Consider what you are asking other Christians to do. Is your going to the mission field your idea? Or God's command? Are you asking for support for yourself or so that you can labor where God wants you? Will their investment result in others being brought into the kingdom of God? Will it result in the growth of Christians? Will it turn people from darkness to light? Then present your need as a challenge for God's people to fulfill their responsibility to "seek first the kingdom of God" with their money. God will add His blessings to their life, that's His part, not yours. Your ministry can provide opportunities for God's people to invest in His work which will result in eternal rewards for them.

Additional blessings can be received by you and your supporters as well, as you pray for one another, accompany one another in the work by means of letters and then share with one another what God has done and is doing when you meet on furlough. You never have that kind of fellowship when you are supported by "pooled funds."

We had occasion to visit one church that contributes to missions through pooled funds. They had no idea who their missionaries were, where they worked, what they were like, or what their problems were. They had never met any of their missionaries. Is that the kind of relationship you want with your supporters? You don't have to beg for support. Present what God has called you to do. He'll do the rest.

Hindrances to Learning the Language

Feelings of Superiority. Learning a language is work. Your mind, jaws, tongue, and whole body become exhausted. You struggle to repeat the strange sounds you are hearing. It is even worse, trying to understand them. Is it worth it? "I will never be able to communicate!" you say. How much better and easier it would be to teach the people English!

Their customs are so strange, too. They do things all wrong. What a task to get these people straightened out! You know all of the nuances of the English language and will never know them of this "new language." Why waste your time adapting everything you are and know to such a backward people? You think, "Will these people be able to appreciate everything I am bringing to them? Do they know what I have gone through to get here?"

Again one has to go back to the reason why he finds himself on a mission field. Are you there to "Americanize" the people? To show what you have learned? To be looked up to as the "Great White Father"? To be eulogized by the people because of who you are and what you have done? Or are you there to follow in the footsteps of One who came "to seek and to save that which was lost"? The only way you can do that is through communication by means of language and life. He who has called you will also bring it to pass. Get yourself, your culture, your superiority out of the way. Let God have *His* way. He will bring you through victoriously for Him. I know. I have seen it happen. I have also seen the reverse. Which way will be your way?

Lacking Discipline. Can you believe that some missionaries get to the field who do not live disciplined lives and who have not even learned good study habits?

How about you? You're not on a mission field—yet. You might be someday. Do you live a disciplined life now? Are your study habits what they should be? Crossing an ocean doesn't solve these problems.

In learning a language, one must give himself—his mind, time, interest, dedication and strength—to learn that new language to the best of the ability that God has given. Failure to do so will seriously affect his future ministry.

The missionary will never have another time to dedicate himself to language study as he will during his first year on the field. He must take full advantage of that opportunity. It pays big dividends. He will experience the reward in his future ministry.

A missionary must also be disciplined in his spiritual life. Unfortunately, some have arrived on the mission field with great expectations, only to return "home" disillusioned. They say they were victims of circumstances. Sometimes there are circumstances beyond human control but too many fail because of a lack of discipline in spiritual living. This is immediately seen in service. Remember, God is in our circumstances. Give yourself to Him—"present your bodies a living sacrifice, holy, acceptable unto God, which is your reasonable service" (Romans 12:1). Be a disciplined Christian—"And be not conformed to this world: but be ye transformed by the renewing of your mind, that ye may prove what is that good, and acceptable, and perfect, will of God" (Romans 12:2). Then watch Him work His will in your life.

Failing to Mix with the People. Preferring the company of missionaries rather than the people to whom you are ministering can be a real barrier to learning a language. It is easy to rationalize. After all, you can't speak the language. You don't know the customs. You don't know the people. You don't want to be embarrassed. You feel lonely. You are making so many adjustments and you don't feel well, neither does your mate nor the children. You're studying, but don't understand what's being said. You're tired and it's just too much of an effort to mix with the people. Yet you do crave companionship.

There are other missionaries nearby. They are going through the same thing that you are. They can help you, and so you go and talk with them. There is nothing wrong in that. You can learn much from them, but you won't learn the language. You'll speak English.

To learn a new language, you must saturate yourself with it and the only way to do that is to talk to the people. Sure, you will make mistakes and be embarrassed. That's natural. It is hard as your mind is tired and your tongue won't work, but the people will appreciate what you are trying to do. The people will help you and you will get to know them better. You will create lasting friendships as you begin to understand some things about them, meeting them in their homes and breaking down barriers. You will begin to identify with them and their way of life. Your understanding of the language will increase in proportion to the way you give yourself to study it.

The ministry of missionaries who spent too much time with Americans when they were studying the language will reflect carry-overs from that time. They will crave American companionship over companionship with nationals. Those who mixed as much as possible with the people, showing themselves friendly, still have friends from those days of language study. They are the missionaries that have the most effective ministry for God among the people of their adopted land.

We recommend that while you are in language study you look for a place of ministry. Get the people to help you. Seek to be used of God to bring others to Christ while you are learning the language.

Fearing Criticism. Some new missionaries actually use the new language as little as possible for fear of criticism. Let's imagine that you are a college and seminary graduate. You have no trouble with English. You can communicate what you feel to whomever you desire at any time. Suddenly you are thrown into a situation where you are virtually a babbling infant. You can't express yourself. You don't understand what is said. You have to ask the person to speak slowly, to repeat. You are embarrassed, and your ego is suffering. You can only talk using nouns, the verbs are impossible and you can't get the order right on the adjectives. Adverbs, they're something else again, and prepositions—forget it! Every time you open your mouth you make a mistake. You feel like a nitwit. So you say, "I won't talk."

One English teacher we had in Brazil couldn't understand why her students didn't learn English. She had taught foreign students in the States and they all had learned. What made the difference? In the States her students HAD to speak English. Everywhere they went English was spoken. Here, they only spoke English in class, so they didn't learn. Language proficiency only comes with use.

Sure, you will make mistakes. Learn to laugh at yourself. Make the adjustment necessary and "carry on." Some people will criticize your use of the language or correct you in such a way that you feel like a dope and say to yourself, "I'll never learn."

Who brings that thought to you? It's your old enemy. Tell him that the One who had to confound the languages of the world because of the sin of the people will help you learn this language so that the message of salvation will bring to the people an opportunity for their sins to be forgiven.

There are always those who are ready to criticize. Accept the criticism and make it constructive for yourself. Make the necessary corrections so that you can more effectively serve the Lord. Criticism can't harm, but your attitude to criticism can!

Hindrances to Living a Normal Life

Letting Loneliness Overcome You. Loneliness and separation are constant hindrances to the living of a happy, normal life on the mission field. Why? Because loneliness isn't normal and requires adjustments to cope with it successfully. It is an ever present need that will plague and destroy if one lets it get the upper hand.

When we say good-bye to family and friends to take up a new life among strangers who will take years to get to know, we are separating ourselves from our childhood love. After many tears, prayers and submission to God, the wound begins to heal and His love fills the emptiness and void left by the absence of one's dear family. God must be to us father, mother, sister and brother. His love must fill our empty hearts so that we can find peace and joy with a new people. This can only come as we can love others, love the new brown faces whose language is so difficult to understand, and make them our family. As we love them, win them, teach them, and see them grow and develop, our loneliness disappears and we find fulfillment and new joy.

The separation from family is only the beginning of many separations. The children grow so rapidly that before we know it the home teaching is no longer adequate. They need the competition of classmates and the social life of an organized school. The mission school is 600 miles away! How can we let them go?

Once they leave, Mom and Dad know that their "normal" home life will never be normal again. Their children will be theirs only during vacations and furloughs for the rest of their lives. Boarding a plane for that first flight to school marks the beginning of the many agonizing good-byes. If we have never stopped to count the cost we do it then, and if it's too great, if loss outbalances gain, we can never be really happy on the mission field. The loneliness and heartache will overcome us and the fact that we've counted the cost too late will be our defeat.

We do have a problem, then, don't we? To me it can be the most critical hindrance to missionary service. Of all the difficulties that we face—unknown illnesses, lack of medical care, attacks from evil spirits, language barriers, etc., there is nothing that compares with the separation from one's children, giving them up to others to mold and train.

If I were to stop here, I would leave you discouraged. So, let's stop looking at today and look beyond. God always rewards a step of faith—faith that enables us to trust and obey, placing our possessions in His care. His reward for faith and obedience is blessing—today, tomorrow, and always. The first blessing comes as He wipes away the tears and replaces anguish with peace. The second blessing comes as we see how He is so much more capable of molding lives than we are and how He so wonderfully answers our prayers. The third blessing comes as we see those who have been given into His care follow Him, and this is the greatest reward of all. Our loneliness is rewarded with His gracious blessings because He is a God who understands and cares.

Holding On to "Things." Have you ever stopped to think how important "things" are to you? Perhaps it is clothing, a home, a musical instrument, television, an automobile, or anything else that has been put into that special category of "special things." It is natural that we have "things" that give us a little comfort or diversion. We North Americans have been brought up with them and they become indispensable to us. When our Heavenly Father lays His hand upon us and asks us to leave the "things" and follow Him, we face a problem. Some will not heed the call for this reason. Others will go to the mission field and there latch onto other "things" that become theirs.

How does this become a hindrance to living a happy normal life on the mission field? I discover, in this new land, that people misuse my "things." They spit on my floor, soil my furniture, break my "pretties," enter any room of my house and meddle in my belongings. This frustrates and angers me and I come to the conclusion that they can just stay away from my house. I'll preach to them and work with them, but the door to my home is closed. However, when I close my door I also close my heart. I shut out my chance for true happiness.

Happiness on the mission field does not come from living in an attractive home and being surrounded with "things." Happiness comes from sharing what I have and what I am with others. Happiness comes from loving and serving. I'm sure that our loving Saviour led a very happy life. He was separated from His Father and had not even a place to lay His head. How could He possibly have been happy? His happiness came from doing the will of God: loving others, meeting their needs, teaching them to love His Father and to be obedient to Him. He had nothing that was His—no "things" to impede His joy, to be broken or stolen. He was supremely happy doing the will of the One who sent Him. Christ left behind Him a trail of contented people who, because of His life of love, also came to know happiness.

What a wonderful example God has given us. He tells us in His Word that we are to be "conformed to the image of his Son" (Romans 8:29). It is easy for us to sing, "I would be like Jesus," but it's quite another thing to be what Jesus was. God has a tremendous amount of patience with us. He knows how attached we become to what is OURS and He continually tries to teach us the right way to live, to give ALL to Him. He wants to take away the love of "things" that hinders our relationships with others and because of this, hinders our happiness.

Resenting the Lack of Social Life. I am a very social person, and while I like to work, I believe that "all work and no play makes Jack a dull boy." I never wanted to fall into the "dull" class. I was brought up in a church that provided social life for its young people. Christian fellowship is great and we, as God's children, need it.

Well, the Lord called me to the mission field. During language study we had many times of fellowship with the other missionaries we met and it was wonderful. I thought, "It's great to be on the mission field serving the Lord with all of these who, as I, have answered the call of God." Well, we finished our language course and went off to our various fields of service. At first I didn't miss the social life because everything was so different. I enjoyed the beautiful blue skies with their fluffy white clouds, the lovely tropical trees and plants, the stars that like shining jewels studded the night skies, and the pets that we soon accumulated. I was fascinated by the strange sights and noises and felt contented in this new culture.

Gradually, however, I became accustomed to the novelties and they were now commonplace to me. The days became full of endless tasks and each night there were too many left undone when I closed my eyes for sleep. I was no longer a newcomer and people expected me to understand everything they said and they wanted to understand me. I had to listen so hard and it was always a mental struggle to go out and face the world. The grind continued day after day and how I longed for a bit of social life. I wanted to go out for a drive and enjoy a delicious hamburger with fries and a shake. I wanted to go someplace and do something! I just felt that I had to get away from it all!

Now, I might have called it quits and gone home discouraged, disillusioned, and frustrated had the Lord not brought my attention to His Word. I looked at the life of the Lord Jesus—my example—who deprived Himself of His beautiful heavenly home, His glory, the praise and adoration that the angels duly gave, and of everything that was His. Instead of being served and worshiped as He was in His own home, He became the servant who ministered to those who were not worthy of His love. He has just one desire and that was that man might come to know His Father.

How can we look at Christ and not see how small and

selfish we are? You can be sure that I asked my Lord to forgive me and He did, and He gave me real joy in facing each new day. He gave me His love and compassion to win those whose language and customs are difficult to understand.

I can't say that I wouldn't like to enjoy a bit of familiar social life now and then, but that can wait until furlough. While I'm here, I want to use every opportunity to make Christ known. When I get to glory I'll really be able to enjoy being in His presence because I've gotten so well acquainted with Him here and have learned how He lives to have me enjoy pleasing Him.

Hindrances to a Rewarding Ministry

Majoring in the Minors. We sometimes ask ourselves these questions: What should I do today? What is most important? What can I leave undone? What is my first responsibility to God? How can we distinguish the "majors" from the "minors"?

This is a problem of life. Many times we don't concentrate on the really important issues. This is a subtlety that Satan likes to use to sidetrack us. What we are doing can be necessary, good, important, and satisfying, but too often we become "cogs" in a machine and play at being Christians. We don't take God seriously.

We need to look at ourselves from God's perspective. He made us and has given us the ability to complete our part in His ministry. We need to learn to use what He has given us. This comes as we establish priorities for our life. These must be established under the direction of the Holy Spirit. Certainly Romans 12:1 and 2 must be considered in this regard. To present ourselves to Him completely should be our first priority. Then we should decide what He wants us to do. This will be determined by our talents, where and how we can best use them, and what results should be seen. This will involve the *establishing of goals* as well as ways to measure our *progress toward those goals*.

We have a world to win. We have a message that transforms. We must present this message in the power of the Holy Spirit so that people will accept Christ. In order to do this we must be partakers of this power—living daily under His control. Our major responsibility to our Lord is to reflect His image to others so that we will attract men and women to Christ by our LIFE.

Hanging On to "Our Way." Believe it or not there *are* other ways of doing things besides "our way." They may be different and not always quite as effective, but that does not make them wrong. We need to find out the reason behind the way things are done in another land instead of immediately trying to change them. Perhaps we are the ones who ought to change. If we take time to try to understand the people and their culture, we will be better able to help bring about a change, should that be necessary.

We should be ready to recognize that their way may be better than ours. Certainly our point of view is more apt to be respected if we have taken time to learn the "why" of the way things are done. We must not let our culture and customs blind us to valuable insights that people have gained through a lifetime of living in their culture. After all, that is the culture that we are adopting. They are not adopting ours.

A fine looking, talented couple came to the field with all the prospects for a successful ministry. They had been a success back home and their board had every confidence in them. Their philosophy was to do things as they always had, the good ole American way. I won't take the time to tell you the whole sad story, but nothing went as they had planned. The nationals too had rights and opinions as well as "know how," and they refused to bend and bow to the desires of the missionary couple. The couple became unhappy, frustrated, and completely disillusioned. They returned to their homeland before completing one term.

We can't transplant a North American church, methods, attitudes, and culture, bag and baggage and expect to do an effective work in another country. We can transplant the saving power of Christ with a heart full of love and learn to adapt and be adaptable.

Lacking Experience in Christian Work. Believe it or not, some missionaries arrive on the field with very little experience in any phase of Christian ministry. They have finished Bible School and Seminary but were so busy putting themselves through school that they didn't have time to get any "practical experience."

Christ didn't just preach to His followers, He trained them. They worked with Him and knew how to do the job required before He sent them out. A missionary is a follower of Christ and is expected to do anything and everything. If he hasn't had practical experience in service, he is unprepared to fulfill his ministry. How can he learn to pastor a church, work with young people, or teach others while he is in a foreign country struggling to learn a new language? This just isn't possible. A missionary needs to get this experience before going to the field so that when he arrives he already knows how to approach the task that Christ has given him to do. No one has any excuse for being unprepared for Christian work today when there are so many opportunities at hand.

Now is the time to prepare yourself for service. Now is the time to overcome those things which could hinder your service for your Lord, wherever He may send you.

CHAPTER 12

Where Are We in Missions Today?

Ralph Covell

Have you ever sung the hymn, "Jesus Shall Reign Where'er the Sun Does His Successive Journeys Run"? Possibly you thought that it was a prophecy for the distant future and you might never live to see it come true. We are not sure when Jesus Christ is going to return and establish His earthly kingdom. We do know, however, that today—for the first time in human history—Jesus is reigning in the lives of His people in every country of the world!

Early Missions

Such an amazing fact would have seemed a dream to that little band of twelve disciples to whom Jesus first gave His command two thousand years ago. They went to the very ends of the then known world—possibly even to Spain—but could only wonder about what lay beyond. In the next few centuries the gospel was carried into North Africa, the Middle East, and some intrepid pioneers reached even India and China. Essentially, however, Christianity was a European religion. During the twelfth and thirteenth centuries the Dominicans and Franciscans, Roman Catholic missionary orders, established many churches in distant China. Three hundred years later another hardy missionary band, the Jesuits led by Francis Xavier, proclaimed the Catholic faith in India, Japan, China and Africa.

The Protestant churches that had come into being in the sixteenth century were slow in catching a missionary vision. Some thought that the Great Commission no longer applied to them; others were not sure how they could do missionary work without missionary orders. But this was Roman Catholic methodology and the reformers did not wish to copy them. And a few of the Protestant Reformers and those who succeeded them in later generations, both in Europe and Great Britain, thought that God would be able to do the task of saving the world without their help.

Modern Missions

This lack of missionary concern was decisively reversed in the last part of the 1700s by a young man named William Carey. A shoe cobbler with little formal education, Carey was truly a "world Christian." Each day as he worked, he pondered the map of the world on his wall. He searched out the statistics to show how much of his world of 730,000,000 did not know the Saviour. By preaching and writing he implored the believers in his generation to form prayer groups, to organize mission societies and to do all in their power to fulfill the Great Commission in their day. Above all, he urged, they must not sit back and wait for God to work. Rather, they must take the initiative and use the "means" that God had placed at their disposal to evangelize the world with the Christian gospel.

Beginning then, which was in about 1800, the Protestant church awoke with a start to the obligation that it had for world evangelism. From that time until the present more people have become Christians than in all of the first eighteen hundred years in the history of the church!

This amazing accomplishment has been possible because of several important factors.

First of all, *God revived His church* in Europe, Great Britain and America so that it had a spiritual concern for people around the world who had never heard the gospel message.

Second, the *Industrial Revolution,* first in Great Britain and then in the United States, provided the means and the financial resources that could be utilized by churches and by Christian nations in the task of world evangelization.

Third, Western nations, sparked by the need for raw materials, markets for their manufactured products, carved up most of the world into their own colonies. And, right or wrong in itself, *colonialization* made it possible politically for messengers of the cross to travel everywhere with much support and only little opposition from governmental power.

As Christian missionaries went out into a world controlled politically and financially by their own governments, God used them to do His will. Their most important task was to preach the gospel, win people to faith in Jesus Christ, and establish Christian churches. Appalled by the many physical and moral needs they saw around them—far more severe than those they had seen in their homelands—they started schools, built hospitals, opened orphanages, fought social problems in society, translated the Bible and prepared and distributed all kinds of Christian literature.

They faced tremendous difficulties: strange and deadly diseases; unhealthy climates; opposition of entrenched non-Christian religions; physical obstacles of jungles, mountains, oceans and deserts; ignorance and superstition; misunderstanding and opposition on the part of peoples totally different from them. Death, defeat, and discouragement was often their lot.

But they also saw God do tremendous things. James Dennis, American Presbyterian missionary to Syria, gave a series of lectures in 1893 at Princeton Seminary, one hundred years after Carey, and reported the following statistics for the world mission of the church: the Bible translated in full or partially into 320 languages, 7800 organized Protestant churches, 900,000 converts with a Christian community of possibly four million, and thousands of missionaries in nearly 17,000 mission stations or sub-stations. All of this in 100 years and yet the best was to come.

Christian missions were given even more impetus during the twentieth century in the recruitment, training and sending of missionary volunteers by the Student Volunteer Movement, the Bible Institute Movement, and the rise of many interdenominational mission boards. Two world wars, a great depression, and the rise of communism, were very disruptive and raised many questions of mission theory and strategy. Yet God continued to reward the faithful service of missionaries and church leaders to the extent that over one-fourth of the world committed itself to the Christian faith. In the words of Kenneth Scott Latourette, a great Baptist historian, it was a period of "Advance Through the Storm."

A milestone of a type was passed in 1946 which brings us into the present period of Christian missions. Previous to World War I, 99.5 per cent of the non-Western world was under Western domination. Beginning largely in the early 1940s the West began to retreat and the structure of colonialism, built up over almost 400 years, came tumbling down within the time span of 25 years. We have seen the virtual end of this within the recent past as Portuguese Guinea, Mozambique and Angola have been granted their independence. Maps of every continent were remade as more than 75 nations entered the United Nations as independent national entities.

Missions Outlook

As we look around the world today, then, we see the church of Jesus Christ in every land (with the possible exception of Mongolia). What is even more important, we see that some of these churches are beginning to send out their own missionaries. When they read the Great Commission of Jesus Christ they believe that it applies to them as much as we think it applies to us. They are not content to witness to their neighbors who are close by, but they wish to go to other countries and to other peoples with the gospel.

A few years ago, when I was in HongKong, I had breakfast with a young pastor in whose marriage service I had participated in Taiwan. As he spoke of the two churches which he directed in that British colony, he told of how the church had been saving money for several years in order that they could send out their own young people as missionaries to many parts of south-east Asia. His last words to me were, "Send me plans or starting a mission society!"

From 1935 to 1965 in Taiwan there was such a tremendous turning to Christ among the Malayo-Polynesian tribal groups that it was called the "Pentecost of the Hills." Thousands were converted to Christ, and hundreds of churches were established. Now some of these Christian churches are participating in the "Burning Bush Mission Society," and their own missionaries are being sent to Kalimantan in Indonesia. This is the same language family to which they belong in

Taiwan, and the probability of their learning the new language better than a Western missionary is much greater. Churches in Korea are planning to send out 1,000 missionaries by 1980.

This is not an entirely new thing. Some churches on "mission fields" were sending out missionaries even in the early 1800s. Only now, however, is this missionary thrust from the "Third World" really beginning to mushroom. (Third World refers to those countries not aligned politically or economically either with the Communist or Western bloc of nations.)

Look, for example, at the most recent statistics of missionaries being sent out by the Third World:

Nigeria	820 missionaries
India	598
Brazil	595
USA (ethnic groups)	448
Philippines	170
Japan	137
South Africa	84
Mexico	69
Oceania	61
Korea	38

Altogether there are 210 sending agencies in 46 countries sending out a total of over 3,000 missionaries (C. Peter Wagner, *Stop the World I Want to Get On,* Regal).

The success story of Christian missions has raised a serious question mark with some people. If the church exists in every country of the world, and if there is continued growth of that church—so that at least in Africa and Latin America it is growing faster percentage-wise than the population in general—and if the church is even sending out its own missionaries, then should we here in America continue to talk about the need for more missionary volunteers? Cannot the church on the "mission field" now care for all of its own needs? Why not begin to think of ourselves for a change—we can put the manpower and the money to good use right here in the concrete jungles of America with all of its open wounds! Let's isolate ourselves from the rest of the world and let them carry on on their own. This strategy, though certainly a logical-sounding one, has been extensively used by some mission societies, and their volunteers and contributions for missions have been reduced drastically over the past ten years. At times their reasoning has been reinforced with the unBiblical assertion that those people who have not heard of Christ are really already saved and, in fact, may be more Christian than those trying to reach them!

If we are going to answer this argument, several facts need to be kept in mind about the need of the world today. First, despite all of the tremendous success of Christian missions and the worldwide missionary outreach of the church, the fact remains that three out of four people in our world are *not* Christians. Second, most of these— about nine out of ten of them—can only be reached by the kind of evangelism that crosses cultural barriers. This kind of evangelism is what we call missions.

As soon as we think about the need of crossing cultural barriers with the message of Christ we see that missions is much more than merely going to every country and crossing the known geographical boundaries. What do we mean?

In nearly every nation—the political unit by which man has divided his world—there are many different "groups of people" or we might even call them "peoples." These "peoples" are separate races, with separate languages, cultural, religious, and social structures.

Think of Taiwan, for example. There is one political

unit—the Republic of China. All the people within this country are citizens of the Republic of China. Culturally, however, you may have many "peoples." The Chinese alone are divided into three major groups—mainland Chinese, Taiwanese, and Hakka—each speaking a different Chinese language. In the mountains are ten groups of Malayo-Polynesian "peoples" with separate languages and cultures. For the church to exist in the political unit of Taiwan says nothing about which of these several groups actually has an effective gospel witness.

In some countries, Nigeria, for example, there are 250 "peoples"—or separate cultural units—and the church has been effectively planted in only five or six of these. If we neglect this fact, we will adopt a wrong strategy and assume that the day of missions is over. If, however, we give proper weight to this important factor, we not only will recognize that the command of Christ has not been fulfilled, but we will pray for the Lord of the harvest to send many more laborers—from His churches everywhere—into these harvest fields.

This is what Jesus said when He commanded His followers to "make disciples of all nations." The Greek term, which most of our Bible versions have translated as "nations," is the word *ethne* from which we derive such English words as ethnic, ethnocentric, etc. It can easily be translated "peoples." We read also from God's Word that in the future there will be those from "every tongue, tribe and people" praising God about the throne of the Lamb. Jesus never intended that we should merely cross political boundaries with the gospel, but that we should reach all "peoples" everywhere with His message.

When we think of the "peoples" of the world, what can we say about them? How many are there? What is their spiritual state? Considerable investigation indicates that the total number of these "peoples" is at least seven hundred. Research by the Summer Institute of Linguistics of "peoples" without the Scripture in their own languages reveals that the number—once thought to be 2,000—may reach four or five thousand. Much more detailed study needs to be done, and this is a central feature of strategy for the future. But the essential picture is clear. Hundreds and perhaps thousands of groups of people numbering nearly 2 1/2 billion have not had an adequate opportunity to respond to Jesus Christ. There is no "near Christian neighbor" to tell them of Christ. Only missionaries from the outside can reach them.

Possibly two-thirds of the unreached are cordoned off behind rather impenetrable political barriers. Communism, nationalism and the revival of traditional religions create problems for the penetration of the gospel. Special strategies utilizing innovative indirect witness by literature, radio, and perhaps television must need to be devised to evangelize them. The local churches in these countries—small and weak though they may be—will need to take much more initiative in evangelizing their own peoples. No clear picture has yet emerged as to the way in which outsiders—the cross-cultural missionary—can contribute the most to the ongoing of God's witness in these relatively "closed" areas. Our most effective weapon will be prayer, both as a means of strengthening God's people in their own witness and in giving wisdom to see how He desires the work to be carried out.

Fully one-third of these unreached "peoples"—over one billion—are, however, accessible to missionary witness. When we think of missions today, a major task is evangelizing these accessible "peoples."

What does this tell us?

We must first recognize that some are generally willing to think about being Christians—they are responsive to Christ. Others have little interest and may be antagonistic—they are resistant. Where people are responsive, the strategy of the future is to be flexible and mobile, to send where God is working in a special way and to concentrate reapers on the ripest harvest fields. The Lord of the Harvest works in different ways, in different places, at different times. To respond to what He is doing in preparing people to follow His Son is the highest kind of strategy. This is to follow the leading of His Spirit.

Where people are not responsive but are resistant, the strategic need is for new attitudes and methods. We need to question, "Why are these 'peoples' resistant?" Is there something fixed in their refusal to consider Christ? Is it that God has allowed Satan to blind their eyes to keep the light of the gospel from reaching them? Has God hardened their hearts? Is the gospel by nature essentially contradictory to all aspects of their culture? Are the reasons only theological—of the nature we have cited—or are there other factors? Is it possible that we have been trying to reap where the need is for sowing the seed? Have we failed to persevere in some fields as we should have?

Another frightening possibility exists. We may have overlooked those cultural and social obstacles that have kept people from receiving Christ. Let's think of Pakistan, for example. This large nation, carved out of India nearly thirty years ago, is 99 per cent Muslim. The small Christian church in the country consists largely of those who were saved out of Hinduism—largely from people who used to be called "outcastes." When they became Christians they rightly brought with them into the church many harmless social and cultural aspects of their past life. Religious words used in their Bible and in their worship reflect this background, as would be expected.

As evangelism has been carried on in Pakistan among the majority Muslim population it has been hoped that any converts from Islam would join this Christian church with its Hindu background. The potential Muslim convert, then, has been faced really with the need for two conversions—a religious one to Jesus Christ and a social and cultural one to the Christian church. Is it not possible that if this second step were removed and Muslim converts could be reached in sufficient numbers within natural family groupings, they could then be organized into local Christian churches that would be more familiar to them in language and worship? The present task in missions demands that we reach the unsaved in the cultures in which they live.

Today, then, is a time when there is a maturing church in every country when mission societies are springing up in "mission fields," and when most of the huge remaining task must be done by crossing boundaries of great cultural difference with the message of Christ. What kind of missionaries are needed for these situations?

The Profile Needed

The missionary for today will have a basic concern for evangelism. Many of the jobs which missionaries did in the past—education, medicine, and social services—are being taken over by governments which do not wish outside organizations, like mission societies, to do these important things. Where missionaries are still involved in this kind of work, they will recognize that the most lasting contribution they can make will be to win men and women to Christ, to strengthen them in their faith, and to teach them how to live as Christians in their own societies. For a world in which three out of four people do not know Jesus Christ, evangelism cannot be given second place.

The proper attitude for today's missionary is that of a servant. He can no longer look upon himself as the leader, the spiritual father, the director of all of the church activities. What were once infant churches have now grown up. Some have established their own mission societies. Increasingly missionaries from the West will work with and under Third World missionaries and the churches they represent. They will not wish to establish their own work or carry out their own plans independently of these churches.

Missionaries of the future must be extremely sensitive men and women. They will be servants not merely of Christ but of those with whom they work. They will be specialists in working with people—not the loner who must do things on his own, but the person who can help others reach their potential, who can take second place, who can let others take the credit.

Americans find it naturally easy to be clumsy bulls in the cultural China closets of the world. Our virtues can easily become vices, if not accompanied with the Biblical ideals of humility, grace, kindness, and understanding. Recently I sat on a committee screening a man and his wife for short-term service in a particular field. This young couple, about to finish their university training, had given the name of a non-Christian professor as one of their references. This professor had some difficulties with the form sent to him by the mission society. Some questions he left blank; others he answered in a hazy way. On one, asking whether this young man had a "concern for souls," he answered that he was uncertain what this meant, but he thought the applicant had it! Most revealing, though, was the brief letter he appended to the reference form. Addressed to the mission society, it noted that the virtures which the mission board desired— boldness, aggressiveness, initiative, the ability to take the lead, etc.—seemed to be those very qualities which might make it difficult for the potential candidate to fit into the target culture, an area of the world in which the professor himself had lived.

This is our problem! Those things which make us Americans—an ability to trailblaze, to pioneer, to lead—unless tempered with the grace of humble servanthood, will disqualify us to be God's missionaries of the future. All missionaries from all cultures are to be leaders—but one leads by serving.

The missionary who serves Christ in another culture today will not only need to develop new attitudes and new relationships, but he must also be prepared to use the new tools and methods which God has given to His people to do His work.

One new tool is research. Is there any way to determine what areas of the world are going to be most responsive to the message of Christ? Do you remember the parable of the sower? The only soil which produced fruit was the good soil. Missionaries have been learning techniques by which they can recognize ahead of time what may be "good soil." They also have been learning more about the way people in other cultures think and what would be the best way to present the gospel message to them.

One missionary in New Guinea, for example, learned that the primitive tribe to which he had gone made peace among their warring factions by exchanging two infants. As long as these two small babies lived there could be no war. He applied this way of thinking to the gospel of Christ. As he explained to the people what the gospel message meant he showed that Jesus was the "Peace Child," given by God to bring peace between Himself and a world that hated Him. And since Jesus lives eternally this peace could not be broken!

Missionaries are learning how to develop better literature, how to prepare more effective radio broadcasts and how to use both traditional and satellite television to beam the gospel message to areas of the world where the missionary himself is not able to go.

Special programs of evangelism have been developed that "saturate" entire countries with the gospel of Christ. Some of these special efforts extend only for several months while others may continue for many years. Church members are given intensive training in how to pray, to visit unsaved friends, and to lead other people to Christ. These campaigns are not only resulting in many new Christians, but they are also producing thousands of new churches each month.

Often these special evangelistic programs are combined with the use of new communication methods. When Luis Palau, noted Latin American evangelist, conducted a large crusade in Managua, Nicaragua, November 1975, his messages were bounded off a satellite over Spain, beamed back in Central America. Dr. Edward Murphy, Latin America Field Director of Overseas Crusades, reported how he stood in the stadium in Managua and heard Palau's voice directly almost at the same time that his earphone picked up the broadcast message that had traveled thousands of miles.

As millions of new converts are made around the world how will they be trained? Some will not know how to read or will read very poorly. For them the American Bible Society has prepared portions of Scripture translation at five different educational levels so that everyone, regardless of his background, might have the joy of reading God's Word. As people learn how to read they are better able to enter local Christian churches and to be taught how to grow in Christ.

For those who desire to be pastors and leaders in the many new churches a new program of theological education has developed in one mission society. Called Theological Education by Extension, this new method of training makes it possible even for older believers with families and with jobs to learn what is needed to pastor a church. They do not go away to school; rather the school comes to them. They usually get together with other students only once a week for a two or three hour period. During the week they have been studying a kind of self-teaching material that makes it possible for them to learn without a teacher being present. Over thirty thousand potential leaders are studying by this method at the present time. What a potential can be found in them for the future of the church of Christ around the world!

Missions has had an exciting past. It has an even more challenging future when all of God's people, including those of us here in America, are called upon to reach out with His redeeming message in the task of world evangelization.